DESTINATION
NEW YORK

Thirty-Third Street and the Empire State Building.

DESTINATION
NEW YORK

Photographs: Detlef Ihlenfeldt
Text: Werner W. Wille

WINDSOR BOOKS
INTERNATIONAL

Manhattan and the south side of Central Park seen from Columbus Circle.

CONTENTS

The view across Manhattan towards the Queensboro Bridge and Queens from the Empire State Building.

NEW YORK – THE SUPER CITY

A Cool Reception

After six long hours we finally touch down at John F. Kennedy Airport. A thousand pictures swirl in the head: the New York skyline, Times Square and Forty-Second Street. Fifth Avenue, Wall Street and Broadway. The Chrysler Building, Statue of Liberty and Guggenheim Museum. SoHo, Greenwich Village and Spanish Harlem. *Last Exit to Brooklyn* and the Manhattan Transfer. Graffiti-covered subway trains and street theatre on Chase Manhattan Plaza. "Welcome to New York?" First of all comes the cold shoulder. After barely setting foot on American soil, an immigration official demands all kinds of information: where one intends to stay, the state of one's finances. At the same time passport stamps are examined with a sceptical expression. It is hardly an encouraging reception and new arrivals leave feeling like someone who has just passed an important examination.

Passengers who come out of the arrivals hall in summer are met by a wall of humidity hitting them like a lead weight. The heavy atmosphere over the city can last for weeks on end, leaving the residents with grey faces and red eyes. Outside John F. Kennedy Airport, in the suburb of Queens, New York seems like any other American town west of the Hudson River. There is no trace of the super city. Buses travel through an everyday landscape with endless boulevards left and right of the Van Wyck Expressway, past monotonous suburbia, giant supermarkets and advertising hoardings. But suddenly the city motorways seem to compress everything and things begin to move quickly. After a last curve, the skyline of Manhattan is visible: the symbol of the new world, a monumental, magical, intimidating sight. But the view is very short-lived as the bus now disappears into a tunnel. A minute later, the new arrival is standing with his luggage in the heart of Manhattan, enveloped by the noise and smell of the street and jostled by passers-by hurrying to and fro. No, New York is not a city which receives the stranger with open arms.

Yet, as though in compensation for the cool reception, it is a pleasure to discover that finding one's way around New York is child's play. There is only Uptown or Downtown, and East or West for the numbered street network. European eyes, surprised by the open perspective in all directions, recognise through the throng of traffic, the shorelines of Brooklyn and Queens to the east, and New Jersey to the west. Is it besser to flutter from one attraction to the next like a butterfly, or to amble like a beetle warmed by a springtime sun feeling its way step by step? Uniquely, New York offers a third way of discovery: the cinema. You don't have to be a cinema addict to stroll any part of Manhattan and come across familiar squares and streets. The film reel is running in Battery Park on the southern tip of Manhattan from where tourists cross over to see the Statue of Liberty, and where employees of the city's brokerages – Wall Street is nearby – eat their lunchtime sandwiches. In the middle of this scene, Madonna and Rosanne Arquette – in "Desperately Seeking Susan" – had their first rendezvous. Countless films have used the Manhattan skyline as a backdrop. The favourite location of film directors is the harbour setting of Brooklyn Heights: Bertolucci in "La Luna," John Huston in "Prizzi's Honor," John Carpenter in "Escape from Manhattan," Wim Wenders in "The American Friend," Ivan Reitman in "Legal Eagles," and many more.

And the bridges of New York! The most filmed of all is the much commended beauty over the East River, the Brooklyn Bridge, which first connected Manhattan with Brooklyn in 1883. In Michael Wadleigh's horror film "Wolfen," the camera captured the silver gleaming spider's web of steel ropes. In "How To Catch A Millionaire," Betty Grable was surrounded by reporters on George Washington Bridge, the only bridge in New York over the Hudson River. The Queensboro Bridge, an imposing steel

The 328-foot/ 99 metre high towers of St. Patrick's Cathedral, the largest Catholic church in the city, are lost today among the skyscrapers of Fifth Avenue. Nevertheless, the cathedral, built in the second half of the last century in the neo-Gothic style, remains an attractive point of contrast.

A shortage of space has necessitated these water tanks being placed on the roof between offices and apartment blocks. Sun and fresh air are rarities on the streets of New York owing to the way buildings have been built extremely close together.

framework structure, had a magical effect in Woody Allen's "Manhattan" through the black and white hues. This masterly director especially understood his city and the mental pain of its residents. His work, and that of the other local directors, like Martin Scorsese, John Cassavetes and Sydney Lumet, always describes a piece of the real New York, not merely by using authentic scenes to shoot the films, but through their connection with the social and cultural uniqueness of the metropolis. Sydney Lumet's hit "Dog Day Afternoon," played out somewhere in Brooklyn, was about the odyssey of an ignorant Uptowner; Scorsese's comedy "After Midnight" wandered through East Village and the gallery quarter of SoHo.

Door To The Promised Land

Films portray New Yorkers as a collection of types who must fit on an assessment scale ranging from "peculiar" to "dangerous to the public". Nowhere else – perhaps with the exception of Rome and Paris, which also have a mythical aura – does one think it possible that the streets are peopled by monsters and all kinds of eccentrics. But in New York, according to

the films, there are bloodthirsty Indians ("Wolfen"), and immortal sword fighters ("Highlander"), while the film "Taxi Driver" created the prototype of the modern city neurotic. The core of these New York films lies is the "everything is possible" credo of the city, and in the principle of "do your own thing".

There is a grain of truth in this: New York offers a sense of freedom. It was felt by the very first settlers – thirty French-speaking Walloon families who moved here in 1624 to escape persecution because of their religious beliefs and who founded the Dutch trading post of New Amsterdam. The same feeling must have overcome the millions of immigrants who fled here over the past two centuries to escape famine and other social catastrophes. Between 1850 and 1905, more than 850,000 East European Jews found a new home here. They were joined by hundreds of thousands of Irish, Italians, Scandinavians and Germans, many of them manual labourers who wanted to escape the grinding poverty brought on by industrialisation. In the record year of 1907, more than one million immigrants were registered passing through Ellis Island, where today there is a museum dedicated to the mass immigration era. Freedom is also what the new immigrants from Puerto Rico,

Columbia, Lebanon, Israel and the Soviet Union seek. Here are also the artists who have left the staleness of their home or countries to seek recognition in New York.

Apart from the 1940s, when it was a short-term haven for refugees of the Nazi era, New York remains the goal of many success-seekers: the entrance to the world's most popular target of immigration. For them the inscription chiselled on the Statue of Liberty still has real meaning: "Send these homeless, tempest-tost to me; I lift my lamp beside the golden door."

Everyday Life: Both Heaven and Hell

As the turntable between the old and new worlds, New York has little room for tranquility and harmony. Everyday life in this city is a constant collision of contradictons, the incompatible and the absurd. Greed and generosity, racism and tolerance are in permanent conflict. While an entire apartment block expressed concern over a stray cat, and the New York Times has complained about the working conditions of the coach horses in Central Park, every winter homeless people freeze because there is nowhere else for them to sleep but on the city's streets. Destitute individuals collect cigarette butts outside the big stores on Fifth Avenue and rats scrabble among the rubbish sacks piled on the side streets. A woman is given an on-the-spot fine of one hundred dollars for failing to clean up the mess left by her poodle on the street, while on a nearby house porch, a junkie injects drugs directly into a vein.

Everyday life in New York consists of small talk with the East Indian man running a newspaper kiosk, the deathly quiet of the banking district after business has finished for the day, as well as the weekend, which for some can be as desolate as a desert. While Manhattan's towers of glass, steel and chrome stretch into the sky, down on the streets the potholes are so deep they can accommodate wastepaper bins. The hysterical howl of police sirens pierces the streets, while contemplative peace can be found in the Japanese tea garden in Brooklyn's Prospect Park. Anything is thinkable, everything is possible in New York. A typical New York paradox is crime. An example: a picture of John Gottis, the city's most noted Mafia boss, on the front page of New York Magazine which carries a story about his career, family and business. Details about the activities of the Mafia and the powerful drug syndicates are noted by

11

New Yorkers like the weather. Nobody seems to be bothered about red plastic capsules found scattered on the pavement on elegant Park Avenue – carelessly tossed away evidence of the addictive drug crack. The police have been helpless for a long time and it is left to privately-organised neighbourhood groups to rid their apartment blocks of dealers and addicts.

Legal versus illegal: in a city where personal success is paramount, there are few real restrictions. An internationally famous nightclub acquires an annual turnover of millions of dollars before someone discovers that the owner does not have a licence to sell liquor. Prostitution is illegal and yet cable television advertises the activity under "dating services". On the other hand, whoever lives in a district controlled by the Mafia need not fear burglaries, and the rubbish collection functions uninterrupted – even during strikes.

What unnerves New Yorkers most is street crime, whether it is attacks on the open street or the subway, rape or burglary. However, New York's record is no worse than average for the United States. What may raise the threshold of fear for New Yorkers is the fact that street life is much more a part of everyday life here than in any other American city. In fear of burglary, New Yorkers have double, even triple locks on their doors, alarms, and even iron bars at the windows of fourth floor apartments. House entrances in the Upper East and West Sides are guarded by porters equipped with walkie-talkies.

Supermarkets have armed guards, thereby creating the impression that wealthy whites – a minority – are in need of being defended. The third and fourth worlds, which most New Yorkers never come face to face with, lie only a couple of subway stops away from Manhattan, in the big slums of Brooklyn and Queens. Most residents would never see the men and women here carrying sacks on their backs or pushing a shopping cart filled with the empty cans and bottles they have fished out of wastepaper bins in order to collect the five-cent deposit. The New Yorker with a reasonable income rarely bothers to take such things back to the shop. But by leaving the deposit for someone else to pick up he kills two birds with one stone: he helps others to earn a sort of living, and frees himself from the worry about their existence.

Vitality and Ethnic Diversity

Unlike, say, Dallas or Los Angeles, life in New York is very much street-orientated, particularly in summer when a tropical heat hangs over the city. This is when people seek relief in the parks, on the beaches or on the steps leading into their homes. And this is when New York's vitality, ethnic and cultural variety, beauty and greatness unfolds.

A sunny Sunday afternoon under a cloudless sky with a fresh breeze blowing in off the Atlantic. On such a day one forgives New York for everything; the whole population seems to be on its feet. In Central Park, there are crowds of joggers, cyclists, strollers and skateboarders. Cars are banned in Central Park, where the only traffic permitted is a couple of horse-drawn carriages for tourists. It is a wonderful place for people to meet and relax. The roller skating regulars meet at the roller rink, and many have brought huge stereo radios – some as large as fridges – tuned into the popular black music station KISS. The atmosphere becomes almost electric with white students from Downtown, the Upper East and West Side, blacks from Harlem, young mothers with their children, Bronx college girls, muscular gays, and black-haired Ragazzi from Brooklyn dressed in colourful rags, all absent-mindedly circling the oval. Beer and ice cream venders as well as the boys with the special cigarettes mingle with the crowds. A strange euphoria engulfs the scene. Who among them would swap this place for anywhere else in the world?

On the big meadow at the southern edge of the park, sun-worshippers gather to acquire a tan, and families and other groups settle down to enjoy picnics. They while away the time until sunset, or until the New York Philharmonic Orchestra gives one of its famous free concerts. When the conductor lifts his baton, one-quarter-of-a-million New Yorkers – people of all races, nationalities and ages – listen.

More than any other city in the United States, New York is a pedestrian's paradise. A knowledgeable person strolling the streets will be able to recognise the different cultural and architectural developments. The neighbourhoods manifest the various ethnic cultures which have grown up in the city. Since New York was first colonised by whites, it has been a centre of immigration: for some a transit camp with all the attendant deprivations, for others a final resting place of hopes for a new life. Eighteen languages were spoken here in 1643, only twenty years after the first colonization. Signs of immigration from all over the world are still identifiable in the names of streets and buildings. One can cross continents within the city. If one wishes to go from China to Italy, one only has to cross Canal Street. It is also just as easy to go from Puerto Rico to Israel. And Greece is found in Astoria in the Queens district.

Manhattan is divided by 110th Street which resembles an uncrossable river. North of this

Competing giants: next to these huge buildings, the old skyscrapers seem small. In the midtown business quarter of Manhattan, numerous towers seem to be trying to topple one another.

Haircutting on the subway platforms for the lines crossing at Seventh Avenue/34th Street.

demarcation line is Harlem, a world closed to whites but whose influence has extended worldwide. This is where jazz, swing and be bop were born. In the 1960s, youngsters danced to soul. Today the music is rap and hip hop. Black theatre and ballet are also at home in Harlem. In Barrio, the quarter west and east of Harlem, Latin America is squashed into a few square miles.

Many cultural traditions have been passed from generation to generation in a conscious effort to maintain some link with ethnic origins. These traditions often surface at the numerous street block parties, which are every bit as colourful as the big parades on Fifth Avenue. Some ethnic families have barely changed their lifestyles from that of their mother countries. In Little Italy, third generation residents speak better Italian than English, and on Sundays the entire community goes to church together. Across narrow Mulberry Street smells of salami, mozzarella and garlic waft through the air and the many street cafés serve espresso and tiramisu. In the Brooklyn district of Brighton Beach – renamed Little Odessa by its Russian residents – one could be on the Black Sea coast: restaurant menus are written in Cyrillic, the waiters speak little if any English and vodka is drunk with meals.

East Village: The Invasion of Big Money

East Village, located between 14th Street in the north, Houston Street to the south, Broadway in the west and the East River in the east, is one of the most interesting quarters of Manhattan. A development is taking place here which in other parts of Manhattan – in Midtown, the Upper East Side, the banking district, and Chelsea – has already been completed. In East Village the process of modifying the ethnic and cultural mix of a district into the New York of the future is already in motion. The face of New York will become more chilly, elegant and cleaner: an antiquated beauty but without heart. The buzzword is gentrification, a process making districts monotonously exclusive.

Sixth Street is the home of many East Indian families. Smells of curry and turmeric drift through the morning air on the streets where an Indian restaurant is certain to be on the next row. A few steps further on, in Third Avenue, there is a Ukrainian enclave. Next to an Orthodox church wedged between two houses, are restaurants which offer evidence of the ethnic character of the neighbourhood: the "Kiev" is open around the clock. On the corner of Ninth Street "Veselka's" produces

wonderful borsch with home-made chala bread. Another traditional East Village group is formed by artists and bohemians. These painters, film-makers, actors, photographers, writers, musicians, designers and hustlers have their own infrastructure of cafés, bars, galleries, boutiques and shops – a stimulating contrast to the introspectiveness of the old, established residents.

A few years ago no one gave a second thought to this area. There was a weekly heroin market, addicts occupied burned-out houses and the police might as well have been on the moon. Only a couple of ruins on the avenues survive as a reminder of this time and soon these, too, will be gone. The area was discovered at the beginning of the 1980s by young, prosperous professionals who moved in with their money and enthusiasm to renovate. The junkies, dreamers, hippies and poverty-stricken – especially the big families who enjoyed low rents – were squeezed out. With them went many small shops and businesses unable to pay the steep rent increases.

Sections of old East Village stubbornly try to hold out against the invasion of big money: street rubbish bins, with their contents spilling over, create a crazy slalom course while pensioners spend their days playing chess in Tomkins Square. Next to them the leftover junkies and alcoholics, undisturbed by the police, have set up makeshift tents strung between the benches. Vitality and creativity still pulsate in the Village where old and new cultures collide in a productive scene only one mile away from the urbane monoculture of the Upper East and West Sides, and the elegant Fifth Avenue. In the end, though, the bohemian idyll with its mix of peoples will become just a memory – the improvised gallery setting new trends behind a shabby façade, special offers starting at fifty cents in second-hand shops, and Polish restaurants with the menus written in two languages.

The Old Jewish Quarter

When you cross Houston Street ("Haustn" in New York dialect), you step over an invisible border into another New York ethnic district. Here, in a southerly direction beyond Delancey Street, many of the men on the streets wear long black coats, black hats and long beards. The schoolboys wear plaits under their yarmulka caps. This is the start of the old Jewish quarter, recognised by the red neon sign – on Houston Street – of a famous restaurant, "Katz's Delicatessen," which has its own butcher. In the shop window, next to the salami and sausages, there are

The arrow straight streets – Fifth Avenue is an example here – make orientation in Manhattan easy. The only exceptions are Broadway, following the route of an old Indian hunting track, and the streets of the former old town on the southern end of the island.

17

thank you letters and signed photographs from presidents, generals and veterans – recipients of Katz's food packets during various American wars.

Little has changed on Hester Street and the surrounding alleys since the days of the silent film of the same name. There are still kosher bakeries producing blintzes and apple pies and enticing shops like "Guss's Pickle Emporium" on Essex Street offering a wide range of pickled vegetables. The stuffed fish can only be recommended for the ethnologist: it tastes like it looks, colourless. But it is well worth trying a bagel with cream cheese and smoked salmon.

Further along in the direction of the East River, in the area of Attorney Street, Latin American faces are more common and Latin American music rings out until late into the night. The Spanish signs *"Se habla yiddish"* (We speak Yiddish) in supermarkets are a good indication that this old quarter is changing its identity.

Faces of the city, where a large slice of life is found on the streets: a sweets vender; cleaning up after celebrations; breakdancing in front of the New York Public Library...

Skyscrapers and Speculators

The relentless way in which districts are subject to rapid change has been going on since the first settlers, Dutch colonists, established New Amsterdam (before the British changed it to New York). Even in 1856, Harper's Magazine wrote: "Whoever returns here after ten years will find nothing, absolutely nothing, of what he once knew." During the city's most dramatic development period, in the middle of the last century when the migration of hundreds of thousands of Europeans began, the business centre of Manhattan moved a mile northwards every ten years. The size and shape of Manhattan Island has changed constantly since the days of the Dutch: through levelling and excavation – in particular to build skyscrapers which otherwise would have simply toppled over into the Hudson and East Rivers. The foundations of the newest development area – Battery City on the southern edge of Manhattan – were made from the excavations for the World Trade Center. Aerial photographs taken in the 1950s, when the island was still surrounded by piers and docks, show Manhattan looking like a gigantic creature. Only a few of these port facilities have survived. The South Street Seaport Museum and the landing dock of the Staten Island ferry now serve as tourist attractions. Living space was always a scarce business commodity on this small island, and right from the earliest days there were profiteers. The first governor of New Amsterdam, Peter Minuit, was also New York's very first speculator. In 1524 he bought the

... Greek specialities; a black policeman and a passerby in conversation; and a cigarette break on a Cadillac. These are just momentary exceptions in an otherwise hectic pace of life.

entire island from the Manhatto Indians for twenty-four dollars. The region of Manhattan from Houston Street to Inwood Hill Park was settled by the city council in 1811 – under pressure from the powerful property market lobby. It is easy to see the profitable motive in building skyscrapers when the price of a piece of land was already sky high one hundred years ago. All the rich New York families – the Astors and Vanderbilts, for example – founded their wealth on property speculation.

This is the industry of the twentieth century (next to drug dealing). New York's newest parvenu is Donald Trump, who built Trump Tower (Fifth Avenue, corner of 52nd Street) with a showy conceit verging on the obscene.

City of the Successful

Other cities have role models or are noted for particular products. For example, Los Angeles is the centre of the American movie industry. But since New York's port and traditional industries have lost their importance (only the textile industry is of any significance today), it has taken on the role of an ideas city, out of which streams an endless range of fads, fashions and dreams. A film industry blossomed here when Hollywood was still an undeveloped colony on the west coast. The first film stars were hired from Broadway. New York serves as both a national and international centre of art, film, music, publishing, advertising, fashion and finance – and drugs. Countless entrepreneurs and career climbers from all over the world would like to take a lucrative bite out of the "Big Apple." In the Downtown area, below 23rd Street, there are more photographers, actors and acresses, dancers, choreographers, writers, designers, promotionalists, models, stock brokers and financiers than in Paris and London combined. With hard work, creativity and a belief in success they strive to reach the top. But only a few – those who become the subject of a New York Magazine title story, for example – arrive at their goal.

Andy Warhol's film "Becoming Rich and Famous" showed how it can be done. Nobody here wants to become old, so that time becomes a scarcer financial commodity than living space, and the twenty-four-hour work day a plain necessity. The city that never sleeps. Whoever succeeds in New York, goes the legend, can be successful everywhere else in the world: Liza Minelli sings "If I can make it there, I can make it anywhere" in the film "New York, New York." If Bob Dylan and David Byrne, Andy Warhol and Keith Haring, Leo Castelli and Mary Boone had

not remained in their home town, it is doubtful they would have been so lucky. They can attribute a large part of their success to the receptive New York public, which is more curious than any other.

Woody Allen's films identify the typical New Yorker perfectly, so long as they are white, nervous, cynical, resigned (as far as life in New York is concerned), optimistic (as far as one's own career is concerned), sporty, open, ready to help, gregarious and unmarried.

Success means everything to them, thus they take all the disadvantages of living in New York in stride. How much more of this must I take, they ask themselves ingenuously, lamenting the falling quality of life: rubbish on the streets, smog, overfilled and late subways, taxi drivers who never know the way, importunate beggars, time lost in bank queues, the cockroaches. But preferably, they like to talk about money. How much a week they earn, how little they can save because of taxes and high rents – one thousand dollars a month for a simple two room apartment in a run-down location is not unusual – how much they pay their shrink, the psycho-analyst. Ten thousand fit this description, but nobody walks into the trap of allowing themselves to be led into a general lament about New York.

In truth, they are proud of their "Big Apple" and the fact that they have achieved the success of living here. New York is their kind of town, they will say: the most wonderful, beautiful, cultivated, and creative place in the world. Which other city has more splendid bridges, famous art museums, crazy discotheques, bigger stores and such an exciting skyline? Where else can you choose every day between the over one-hundred-eighty-five theatre performances, which other city has so many cinemas on offer and fifteen miles of beach? This is a place of total pleasure and entertainment: to look down on the city from the highest wine bar in the world on the 110th floor of the World Trade Center, or dine on a yacht with the city skyline as a backdrop, or visit the fair on Coney Island, or be present at the opening of an art exhibition.

No other city can offer so much and at any time. Whenever any new fashion or idea finds its way on to the market, there is almost always certain to be a New Yorker involved. Be bop and cool jazz in the 1950s, vogue dancing and pop art in the 1960s, art rock and no wave in the 1970s, performance-theater and hip hop, designer jeans and designer drugs, loft apartments, yuppies, graffiti and gentrification – all made in New York. And while the rest of the world is discussing or adopting the latest craze or fashion, New York is already in search of the next thrill.

New York can always give an insight into what the future holds. An whether it is an assurance of good or a foreboding of something more sinister, it is the unprejudiced judgement of the city's residents. Only one thing is certain here: New York is always fascinating. Welcome to the "Big Apple".

OF DREAMS AND NIGHTMARES
Memories of New York

For most of its history, New York has held a paradoxical position in relation to the rest of the United States. It considers itself to be the only true American city, yet it constantly demonstrates its distinctiveness from the country's other cities. New York's individuality is connected, in part, to the contribution made by the millions of immigrants who have made their home in the city. In the following pages, the experiences described by some of those who flocked to New York over the last hundred years – Europeans, southern Negroes, Puerto Ricans – give some inside views of "the melting pot", the metropolis' fusion of traditions, memories, aspirations and dreams. But, the cultural and economic freedom which characterised the New York of the 1920s has been largely displaced today, leaving instead racial prejudices and socially-marginalized elements. It is such extremes that have always existed in New York, which never cease to excite and challenge the spectator.

The City and Its People

It was silent, the city of my dreams, marble and serene, due perhaps to the fact that in reality I knew nothing of crowds, poverty, the winds and storms of the inadequate that blow like dust along the paths of life. It was an amazing city, so far-flung, so beautiful, so dead. There were tracks of iron stalking through the air, and streets that were as cañons, and stairways that mounted in vast flights to noble plazas, and steps

New York's streets are transformed at night into a sea of neon. It's a time for pleasure – for example here on 57th Street, near Broadway. But the New York police are always at the party.

that led down into deep places where were, strangely enough, underworld silences. And there were parks and flowers and rivers. And then, after twenty years, here it stood, as amazing almost as my dream, save that in the waking the flush of life was over it. It possessed the tang of contests and dreams and enthusiasms and delights and terrors and despairs. Through its ways and cañons and open spaces and underground passages were running, seething, sparkling, darkling, a mass of beings such as my dream-city never knew.

The thing that interested me then as now about New York – as indeed about any great city, but more definitely New York because it was and is so preponderantly large – was the sharp, and at the same time immense, contrast it showed between the dull and the shrewd, the strong and the weak, the rich and the poor, the wise and the ignorant. This, perhaps, was more by reason of numbers and opportunity than anything else, for of course humanity is much the same everywhere. But the number from which to choose was so great here that the strong, or those who ultimately dominated, were so very strong, and the weak so very, very weak – and so very, very many.

I once knew a poor, half-demented, and very much shriveled little seamstress who occupied a tiny hall-bedroom in a side-street rooming-house, cooked her meals on a small alcohol stove set on a bureau, and who had about space enough outside of this to take three good steps either way.

"I would rather live in my hall-bedroom in New York than in any fifteen-room house in the country that I ever saw," she commented once, and her poor little colorless eyes held more of sparkle and snap in them than I ever saw there, before or after. She was wont to add to her sewing income by reading fortunes in cards and tea-leaves and coffee-grounds, telling of love and prosperity to scores as lowly as herself, who would never see either. The color and noise and splendor of the city as a spectacle was sufficient to pay her for all her ills.

And have I not felt the glamour of it myself? And do I not still? Broadway, at Forty-second Street, on those selfsame spring evenings when the city is crowded with an idle, sightseeing cloud of Westerners; when the doors of all shops are open, the windows of nearly all restaurants wide to the gaze of the idlest passer-by. Here is the great city, and it is lush and dreamy. A May or June moon will be hanging

like a burnished silver disc between the high walls aloft. A hundred, a thousand electric signs will blink and wink. And the floods of citizens and visitors in summer clothes and with gay hats; the street cars jouncing their endless carloads on indifferent errands; the taxis and private cars fluttering about like jeweled flies. The very gasoline contributes a distinct perfume. Life bubbles, sparkles; chatters gay, incoherent stuff. Such is Broadway.

And then Fifth Avenue, that singing, crystal street, on a shopping afternoon, winter, summer, spring or fall. What tells you as sharply of spring when, its windows crowded with delicate effronteries of silks and gay nothings of all description, it greets you in January, February and March? And how as early as November again, it sings of Palm Beach and Newport and the lesser or greater joys of the tropics and the warmer seas. And in September, how the haughty display of furs and rugs, in the same avenue, and costumes de luxe for ball and dinner, cry out of snows and blizzards, when you are scarcely ten days back from mountain or seaside. One might think, from the picture presented and the residences which line the upper section, that all the world was inordinately prosperous and exclusive and happy.

And yet, if you but knew the tawdry underbrush of society, the tangle and mat of futile growth between the tall trees of success, the shabby chambers crowded with aspirants and climbers, the immense mansions barren of a single social affair, perfect and silent!

THEODORE DREISER (1871–1945) describes New York between 1900 and 1915 in his book The Color of a Great City. *As with all of his works, the 1923 text is noted for its realistic portrayal of a lifestyle and environment.*

The Real New Yorker

My dear Theodore, – You know – for we have talked it over often enough – that I do not hold you to be a typical New Yorker, since you come of Dutch stock, and first saw the light here on Manhattan Island, whereas the typical New Yorker is born of New England parents, perhaps somewhere west of the Alleghanies. You know, also, that often the typical New Yorker is not proud of the city of his choice, and not so loyal to it as we could wish. He has no abiding concern for this maligned and misunderstood town of ours; he does not thrill with pride at the sight of its powerful and irregular profile as he comes back to it across the broad rivers; nor is his heart lifted up with joy at the sound of its increasing roar, so suggestive and so stimulating. But we have a firm affection for New York, you and I, and a few besides; we like it for what it is; and we love it for what we hope to see it.

This note, addressed to Theodore Roosevelt, was written as the dedication for BRANDER MATTHEWS' 1894 book Vignettes of New York. *The condescending tone of his address is present throughout his book combined with melodramatic and romantic depictions of life in the ghetto. However, on one or two occasions, he manages to present a realistic description of the hardships of everyday life.*

First Glimpse

The swelling caravan of immigration reached its record volume in 1907 when the incoming tide brought to America 1,285,349 aliens. I was one of them, a ten year old boy.

My first impressions of the new world will always remain etched in my memory, particularly that hazy October morning when I first saw Ellis Island. The steamer *Florida,* fourteen days out of Naples, filled to capacity with sixteen hundred natives of Italy, had weathered one of the worst storms in our captain's memory; and glad we were, both children and grown-ups, to leave the open sea and come at last through the Narrows into the Bay.

My mother, my stepfather, my brother Giuseppe, and my two sisters, Liberta and Helvetia, all of us together, happy that we had come through the storm safely, clustered on the foredeck for fear of separation and looked with wonder on this miraculous land of our dreams.

Giuseppe and I held tightly to stepfather's hands, while Liberta and Helvetia clung to mother. Passengers all about us were crowding against the rail. Jabbered conversation, sharp cries, laughs and cheers – a steadily rising din filled the air. Mothers and fathers lifted up the babies so that they too could see, off to the left, the Statue of Liberty. ...

I looked at that statue with a sense of bewilderment, half doubting its reality. Looming shadowy through the mist, it brought silence to the decks of the *Florida.* This symbol of America – this enormous expression of what we had all been taught was the inner meaning of this new country we were coming to – inspired awe in the hopeful immigrants. Many older persons among us, burdened with a thousand memories of what they were leaving behind, had been openly weeping ever since we entered the narrower waters on our final approach toward the unknown. Now somehow steadied, I suppose, by the concreteness of the symbol of America's freedom, they dried their tears.

Directly in front of the *Florida,* half visible in the faintly-colored haze, rose a second and even greater challenge to the imagination.

"Mountains!" I cried to Giuseppe. "Look at them!"

"They're strange," he said, "why don't they have snow on them?" He was craning his neck and standing on tiptoe to stare at the New York skyline.

Stepfather looked toward the skycrapers, and, smiling, assured us that they were not mountains but buildings – "the highest buildings in the world."

On every side the harbor offered its marvels: tugs, barges, sloops, lighters, sluggish freighters and giant ocean liners – all moving in different directions, managing, by what seemed to us a miracle, to dart in and out and up and down without colliding with one another. They spoke to us through the varied sounds of their whistles, and the *Florida* replied with a deep echoing voice.

Bells clanged through our ship, precipitating a new flurry among our fellow-passengers. Many of these people had come from provinces far distant from ours, and were shouting to one another in dialects strange to me. Everything combined to increase our excitement, and we rushed from deck to deck, fearful lest we miss the smallest detail of the spectacle.

Finally the *Florida* veered to the left, turning northward into the Hudson River, and now the incredible buildings of lower Manhattan came very close to us. ...

I felt resentment towards this Ellis Island ahead of us, where we could already see many people crowded into a small enclosure. It could not be a good place. It would have been better if we had stayed in our comfortable home in the Abruzzi, back in Italy. To come here made mother cry. I looked around the deck and saw that many women were crying.

Our little vessel coasted into the slip at Ellis Island. The passengers began to move. We moved with them and as we stepped from the gangplank to the land, all silent and subdued, I knew that my parents were thinking as I was, "What is next?"

The Italian-American writer EDWARD CORSI portrays here the experience shared by millions of immigrants on their arrival in New York – the mixture of fascination and fear on seeing this huge metropolis.

World famous Times Square at the junction of Seventh Avenue and Broadway is the centre of New York's theatre district. Theatres and cinemas showing film premieres crowd together next to countless restaurants and bars. Hundreds of illuminated advertising signs transform the theatre mile at night into a pleasure park.

The Newly-Arrived Immigrant

Ten minutes' walk brought me to the heart of the Jewish East Side. The streets swarmed with Yiddish-speaking immigrants. The sign-boards were in English and Yiddish, some of them in Russian. The scurry and hustle of the people were not merely overwhelmingly greater, both in volume and intensity, than in my native town. It was of another sort. The swing and step of the pedestrians, the voices and manner of the street peddlers, and a hundred and one other things seemed to testify to far more self-confidence and energy … than did the appearance of the crowds in my birthplace.

The great thing was that these people were better dressed than the inhabitants of my town. The poorest-looking man wore a hat (instead of a cap), a stiff collar and a necktie, and the poorest woman wore a hat or a bonnet.

The appearance of a newly arrived immigrant was still a novel spectacle on the East Side. Many of the passers-by paused to look at me with wistful smiles of curiosity.

"There goes a green one!" some of them exclaimed.

The sight of me obviously evoked reminiscences in them of the days when they had been "green ones" like myself. It was a second birth that they were witnessing, an experience which they had once gone through themselves and which was one of the greatest events in their lives.

"Green one" or "greenhorn" is one of the many English words and phrases which my mother-tongue has appropriated in England and America. Thanks to the many millions of letters that pass annually between the Jews of Russia and their relatives in the United States, a number of these words have by now come to be generally known among our people at home as well as here. In the eighties, however, one who had not visited any English-speaking country was utterly unfamiliar with them. And so I had never heard of "green one" before. Still, "green," in the sense of color, is Yiddish as well as English, so I understood the phrase at once, and as a contemptuous quizzical appellation for a newly arrived, inexperienced immigrant it stung me cruelly. As I went along I heard it again and again. Some of the passers-by would call me "greenhorn" in a tone of blighting gaiety, but these were an exception. For the most part it was "green one" and in a spirit of

sympathetic interest. It hurt me, all the same. Even those glances that offered me a cordial welcome and good wishes had something self-complacent and condescending in them. "Poor fellow! he is a green one," these people seemed to say. "We are not, of course. We are Americanized."

For my first meal in the New World I bought a three-cent wedge of coarse rye bread, off a huge round loaf, on a stand on Essex Street. I was too strict in my religious observances to eat it without first performing ablutions and offering a brief prayer. So I approached a bewigged old woman who stood in the doorway of a small grocery-store to let me wash my hands and eat my meal in her place. She looked old-fashioned enough, yet when she heard my request she said, with a laugh:

"You're a green one, I see." …

My intention was to take a long stroll, as much in the hope of coming upon some windfall as for the purpose of taking a look at the great American city. Many of the letters that came from the United States to my birthplace before I sailed had contained a warning not to imagine that America was a "land of gold" and that treasure might be had in the streets of New York for the picking. But these warnings only had the effect of lending vividness to my image of an American street as a thoroughfare strewn with nuggets of the precious metal. Symbolically speaking, this was the idea one had of the "land of Columbus." It was a continuation of the widespread effect produced by stories of Cortes and Pizarro in the sixteenth century, confirmed by the successes of some Russian emigrants of my time.

I asked the grocery-woman to let me leave my bundle with her, and, after considerable hesitation, she allowed me to put it among some empty barrels in her cellar.

I went wandering over the Ghetto. Instead of stumbling upon nuggets of gold, I found signs of poverty. In one place I came across a poor family who – as I learned upon inquiry – had been dispossessed for non-payment of rent. A mother and her two little boys were watching their pile of furniture and other household goods on the sidewalk while the passers-by were dropping coins into a saucer placed on one of the chairs to enable the family to move into new quarters.

What puzzled me was the nature of the furniture. For in my birthplace chairs and a couch like those I now saw on the sidewalk would be a sign of prosperity. But then anything was to be expected of a country where the poorest devil wore a hat and a starched collar.

I walked on.

The exclamation "A green one" or "A greenhorn" continued. If I did not hear it, I saw it in the eyes of the people who passed me.

ABRAHAM CAHAN's famous 1917 novel The Rise of David Levinsky, *considered a classic of the Jewish immigrant experience in New York, critically depicts the Americanization of the protagonist. It also provides a detailed picture of the New York Jewish scene in the early twentieth century.*

Haunted by the Past

Herman Broder turned over and opened one eye. In his dreamy state, he wondered whether he was in America, in Tzivkev, or in a German camp. He even imagined himself hiding in the hayloft in Lipsk. Occasionally all these places fused in his mind. He knew he was in Brooklyn, but he heard Nazis shouting. They were jabbing with their bayonets, trying to flush him out, while he pressed deeper and deeper into the hay. The blade of a bayonet touched his head.

Full awakening required an act of volition. "Enough!" he told himself, and sat up. It was mid-morning. Yadwiga had been dressed for some time. In the mirror on the wall opposite the bed he caught sight of himself – face drawn, his few remaining hairs, once red, now yellowish and streaked with grey. Blue eyes, piercing yet mild, beneath dishevelled eyebrows, nose narrow, cheeks sunken, the lips thin. ...

He got up and went to the window. A few blocks away, the ocean heaved. From the Boardwalk and Surf Avenue came the noises of a Coney Island summer morning. Yet, on the little street between Mermaid and Neptune Avenues, everything was quiet. A light breeze was blowing; a few trees grew there. Birds twittered in the branches. The incoming tide brought with it a smell of fish, and something undefinable, a stench of putrefaction. When Herman put his head out of the window, he could see old shipwrecks that had been abandoned in the bay. Armoured creatures had attached themselves to the slimy hulls – half alive, half sunk in primeval sleep. ...

The house in which Herman lived with Yadwiga was an old building. Many elderly refugee couples who needed fresh air for their health had settled there. They prayed in the little synagogue nearby and read the Yiddish papers. On hot days they brought benches and folding chairs out on the street and sat around chatting about the old country, their American children and grandchildren, about the Wall Street crash in 1929, about the cures worked by steam baths, vitamins, and mineral waters at Saratoga Springs. ...

Even if he never had had a large appetite, the hunger of the Nazi years had left Herman with a sense of excitement at the sight of food. Sunlight fell on crates and bushel baskets of oranges, bananas, cherries, strawberries, and tomatoes. Jews were allowed to live freely here! On the main avenue and on the side streets, Hebrew schools displayed their signs. There was even a Yiddish school. As Herman walked along, his eye sought hiding places in case the Nazis were to come to New York. Could a bunker be dug somewhere nearby? Could he hide himself in the steeple of the Catholic church? He had never been a partisan, but now he often thought of positions from which it would be possible to shoot.

On Stillwell Avenue, Herman turned right, and the hot wind struck him with the sweet smell of popcorn. Barkers urged people into amusement parks and side shows. There were carousels, shooting galleries, mediums who would conjure the spirits of the dead for fifty cents. At the subway entrance, a puffy-eyed Italian was banging a long knife against an iron bar, balling out a single word again and again, in a voice that carried over all the tumult. He was selling cotton candy and soft ice cream that melted as soon as it was put into a cone. On the other side of the Boardwalk, the ocean sparkled beyond a swarm of bodies. The richness of colour, the abundance, the freedom – cheap and shoddy as everything was – surprised Herman each time he saw it.

ISAAC BASHEVIS SINGER (1904 – 1991), a Polish Jew who devoted himself to literature, joined his brother in the United States in 1935, working as a journalist. This depiction of life for a Jew in New York is unusual for Singer, whose writing is set chiefly in the history and culture of the old country.

A New Home for Negroes

Confronted suddenly by daylight, King Solomon Gillis stood dazed and blinking. The railroad station, the long, white-walled corridor, the impassible slot-machine, the terrifying subway train – he felt as if he had been caught up in the jaws of a steam-shovel, jammed together with other helpless lumps of dirt, swept blindly along for a time, and at last abruptly dumped.

Prometheus, of Greek mythology fame, in front of the 70-storey RCA Building. The Radio Corporation of America belongs to the Rockefeller Center, which covers an area equal to three street blocks, making it the largest building complex in the world.

Light and shadow in competition: attractions and problems of a vertically-built city.

The Guggenheim Museum building, an original work of modern architecture, is as worth viewing as the ever-changing exhibitions inside. The museum, on Fifth Avenue, was built during the 1950s with money donated by the late Solomon R. Guggenheim.

There had been strange and terrible sounds: "New York! Penn Terminal – all change!" "Pohter, hyer, pohter, suh?" Shuffle of a thousand soles, clatter of a thousand heels, innumerable echoes. Cracking rifle-shots – no, snapping turn-stiles. "Put a nickel in!" "Harlem? Sure. This side – next train." Distant thunder, nearing. The screeching onslaught of the fiery hosts of hell, headlong, breath-taking. Car doors rattling, sliding, banging open. "Say, wha' d'ye think this is, a baggage car?" Heat, oppression, suffocation – eternity – "Hundred'n turdy-fif' next!" More turnstiles. Jonah emerging from the whale.

Clean air, blue sky, bright sunlight.

Gillis set down his tan-carboard extension-case and wiped his black, shining brow. Then slowly, spreadingly, he grinned at what he saw: Negroes at every turn; up and down Lenox Avenue, up and down One Hundred and Thirty-fifth Street; big, lanky Negroes, short, squat Negroes; black ones, brown ones, yellow ones; men standing idle on the curb, women … trudging reluctantly homeward, children rattle-trapping about the sidewalks; here and there a white face drifting along, but Negroes … every-where. There was assuredly no doubt of his where-abouts. This was Negro Harlem.

Back in North Carolina Gillis had shot a white man and, with the aid of prayer and an automobile, probably escaped a lynching. Carefully avoiding the railroads, he had reached Washington in safety. For his car a Southwest bootlegger had given him a hundred dollars and directions to Harlem; and so he had come to Harlem.

Ever since a travelling preacher had first told him of the place, King Solomon Gillis had longed to come to Harlem. The Uggams were always talking about it; one of their boys had gone to France in the draft and, returning, had never got any nearer home than Harlem. And there were occasional "colored" newspapers from New York: newspapers that mentioned Negroes without comment, but always spoke of a white person as "So-and-so, white." That was the point. In Harlem, black was white. You had rights that could not be denied you; you had privileges, protected by law. And you had money. Everybody in Harlem had money. It was a land of plenty. Why, had not Mouse Uggam sent back as much as fifty dollars at a time to his people in Waxhaw?

The shooting, therefore, simply catalyzed whatever sluggish mental reaction had been already directing

The airy Museum of Modern Art, on 53rd Street, was built in 1939. In addition to its permanent exhibition of modern paintings and sculpture, the museum regularly stages a variety of special exhibitions.

King Solomon's fortunes toward Harlem. The land of plenty was more than that now: it was also the city of refuge.

Casting about for direction, the tall newcomer's glance caught inevitably on the most conspicuous thing in sight, a mignificient figure in blue that stood in the middle of the crossing and blew a whistle and waved great white-gloved hands. The Southern Negro's eyes opened wide; his mouth opened wider. If the inside of New York had mystified him, the outside was amazing him. For there stood a handsome, brass-buttoned giant directing the heaviest traffic Gillis had ever seen; halting unnumbered tons of automobiles and trucks and wagons and pushcarts and street-cars; holding them at bay with one hand while he swept similar tons peremptorily on with the other; ruling the wide crossing with supreme self-assurance; and he, too, was a Negro!

Yet most of the vehicles that leaped or crouched at his bidding carried white passengers. One of these overdrove bounds a few feet and Gillis heard the officer's shrill whistle and gruff reproof, saw the driver's face turn red and his car draw back like a threatened pup. It was beyond belief – impossible. Black might be white, but it couldn't be that white!

"Done died an' woke up in Heaven," thought King Solomon, watching, fascinated; and after a while, as if the wonder of it were too great to believe simply by seeing, "Cullud policemans!" he said, half aloud; then repeated over and over, with greater and greater conviction, "Even got cullud policemans – even got cullud –"

RUDOLPH FISHER was an important black writer of the Harlem Renaissance of the 1920s. His story The City of Refuge *captures the vision of the racial mobility and equality Harlem embodied for those fleeing persecution and poverty in the South.*

An Education Begins

In New York I became an eagle, claws scratching the skin of its gritty sidewalks, wings spread, touching sun, casting shadows on the moon. Hunger glistened in my eyes, beat a war dance inside my veins. Unfamiliar, demanding appetites rumbled across the plain of my heart. I soared, wrestled with the clouds, the echo of my song trailing in the wind.

Wanda and I made the trek together, she to study acting at New York University, I to enter the world of journalism through Columbia's hallowed halls.

Manhattan's western skyline: an "oldtimer" – the 1913 Woolworth Building – between the twin towers of the World Trade Center (right).

Colour in the grey everyday life of New York: graffiti in the subway station on 69th Street/Woodside Avenue in Queens . . .

Looking over our shoulders, the past seemed simple, sure. Turning to face the present, we remembered neither of us had trained for walking tightropes. But when we measured the distance of the drop, balance steadied our stride, stopped blood from the bitten lip.

We shared a one-bedroom apartment with six thousand New York City roaches. The space pressed around us, an inhospitable womb. Drab, worn linoleum was pasted to the floors. The bathroom squatted in a corner of the sloping, L-shaped kitchen. Dingy mustard-colored walls gave the space the atmosphere of a cave. Two hundred dollars' worth of grates, bars, and locks at the windows kept out robbers and the sun.

A young saxophonist from Atlanta lived next door in a room the size of our toilet. Small and wiry, he throbbed with a talent that bled in his eyes. His existence was improvised. One week a gig with Mingus at the Village Gate, then two weeks of shoulders hunched, pounding the street for work. He told us we reminded him of his sisters back home. For him we were a touchstone, an echo of what he'd left behind, so he broke bread with us many nights. Serene and comforting, he basked in the lushness of our articulation, asking, "Sister mine, what was that

word? Run it past me again." Brows clenched in concentration, he spoke best with his instrument. Watching his face open like a Chinese fan, listening to the notes, we heard all we needed to know. Love, hate, wrenched from safe harbour, pushed through gleaming horn holding our awed reflection. His music knitted a life, a lifetime in the shape of a rainbow across the kitchen's stagnant air.

The frustrating, exhilarating getting of knowledge was what New York City, and especially Columbia, was about. I left A.U. with answers suitable for essay questions on midterm examinations, but they crumbled, gasping and inadequate, under the glare of an unpredictable "real" world. Columbia, however, taught something ultimately more important. Columbia imparted an attitude, and drilled not just confidence but fearlessness into its chosen few. The most important thing I learned there was how people get power and who decides who will share it. The curriculum was an obstacle course that used New York City as one large breaking story, a part of which we covered every day.

In her autobiography, MARITA GOLDEN describes the impressions of a young woman from the South moving to New York to begin her studies in

journalism. During her stay in New York she learned what it meant to be black in the twentieth century.

Immigrants and Artists

The greater part of New York is as soulless as a department store; but Greenwich Village has recollections like ears filled with muted music and hopes like sightless eyes straining to catch a glimpse of the Beatific Vision.

On the benches in the square men and women resting; limbs wide-flung, arms pendent, listless; round the fountains and on the corners children, dark-eyed Italian children shrieking now with Yankee-cockney accent, a moment later whispering to their deep-bosomed mothers in the Tuscan of Dante. Here a bunch of Jewish girls like a nosegay, there a pair of Norwegian emigrants, strong of figure and sparing of speech; a colored girl on the sidewalk jostles a Japanese servant and wonders whether he too is colored or is he thought to be white like "dem Dagos."

On every corner you can see a new type; but strange to say no Americans are to be discovered anywhere. New York is the meeting place of the peoples, the only city where you can hardly find a typical American.

The truth has never been penned about Washington Square and Greenwich Village – names which are not synonymous. …

In reality, Washington Square and Greenwich Village are not one. They have become one above the pavement at the height where men's heads pass; but measured out in plain city blocks the Village does not run past Sixth Avenue. It begins somewhere around Twelfth Street and commits suicide at the Battery.

There are as many artists living off the Square as on it. Some shops are mentioned as these artists are mentioned, because they have caught a certain something that for want of a better word we call atmosphere!

We always speak of Daisy Thompson's shop, of the "Treasure Box," of the "Village Store" and of the "Oddity Cellar" – just as many pretty things, however, are to bee seen in a small shop on Eighth Street between Fifth and Sixth Avenues. Why is it not also mentioned? Because it is in, and not of, the Village.

There is the pleasant night life of the Café Lafayette. The Brevoort is loved for its basement, where one can catch the lights gleaming between the shrubbery. There too is the waiter who has been serving you for ten years past. There is a certain familiarity in everything you eat. You can tell just where you are by closing your eyes. The cold cuts of the Lafayette are superior to those of the Brevoort; the New Orleans "Fizzes" are abominable at the latter and delightful at the former. There is a chance that you may meet someone you do not like as there is a probability that you will meet someone that you do. You decide beforehand what kind of a sneer you are going to throw Billy, just how coldly you are going to look past Bobbie or freeze the spinal column of Louise, who has been your next door neighbor for months.

DJUNA BARNES (1892 – 1982) was a New York-born writer whose early fiction and non-fiction stories were set in the Bohemian world of New York. Her novel Nightwood *(1936) has long established itself as a cult novel of this century, and is respected around the world.*

The Jazz Age

Twilights were wonderful just after the war. They hung above New York like indigo wash, forming themselves from asphalt dust and sooty shadows under the cornices and limp gusts of air exhaled from closing windows, to hang above the streets with all the mystery of white fog rising off a swamp. The far-away lights from buildings high in the sky burned hazily through the blue, like golden objects lost in deep grass, and the noise of hurrying streets took on that hushed quality of many footfalls in a huge stone square.

Through the gloom people went to tea. On all the corners around the Plaza Hotel, girls in short squirrel coats and long flowing skirts and hats like babies' velvet bathtubs waited for the changing traffic to be suctioned up by the revolving doors of the fashionable grill. Under the scalloped portico of the Ritz, girls in short ermine coats and fluffy, swirling dresses and hats the size of manholes passed from the nickel glitter of traffic to the crystal glitter of the lobby.

In front of the Lorraine and the St Regis, and swarming about the mad-hatter doorman under the warm orange lights of the Biltmore façade, were hundreds of girls with marcel waves, with colored shoes and orchids, girls with pretty faces, dangling powder boxes and bracelets and lank young men from their wrists – all on their way to tea. At that time, tea was a public levee. There were tea personalities – young leaders who, though having no claim to any particular social or artistic distinction, swung after them long strings of contemporary silhouettes like a game of crack-the-whip. Under the somber, ironic parrots of the Biltmore the halo of golden bobs absorbed the light from heavy chandeliers, dark heads lost themselves in corner shadows, leaving only the rim of young faces against the winter windows – all of them scurrying along the trail of one or two dynamic youngsters.

ZELDA FITZGERALD captured the essence of America's Jazz Age in her short stories, as did her well-known husband F. Scott. "A Millionaire's Girl" first appeared in The Saturday Evening Post, *7 May 1930, depicting the lifestyle of the New York hotel set of the late 1920s.*

Marooned

North Brother Island is a small patch of land just ten minutes out in the East River by the ferry that takes you from 134th Street. The island is in reality, if not geographically, part of the world of Spanish Harlem. It houses the Riverside narcotics hospital for treatment of addicts under the age of twenty-one.

New York City has a ferry ride for everyone, and even if never taken, it is known and made a part of the life of that particular group. Lovers in Greenwich Village read Edna St. Vincent Millay and take the ferry to Staten Island; tourists read "Give me your tired, your poor" and take the ferry to the Statue of Liberty; kids in East Harlem hear the terrible neighborhood maxim on the fate of the addict – "Once a junkie, always a junkie" – and, in hope and desperation, take the ferry to Riverside.

"Julio," a brown and handsome boy of seventeen who lives on 100th Street, took it for the second time in his life after getting an overdose of heroin. He had just served seventeen days in jail for being caught with three guys on a roof with "the works" – the syringe and needle used for injections of the drug. They had heard the cops coming and had thrown away the "stuff" – the heroin itself – but they still had the works and were sent to jail. When Julio got out he went for a fix and was given a powerful overdose that sickened him and, with the urging of friends, led him back to Riverside.

This brief description of life in the Puerto Rican ghetto by DAN WAKEFIELD succinctly grasps the poverty, exploitation and despair these people often suffer, and the one means of escape often employed, drug addiction. Here, the isolation of the drug addicts in society is evoked in their geographical segregation within New York.

Baseball – the city's most loved sport – played by youths in a typically paved and enclosed backyard, here on Sixth Avenue.

The Lower East Side, today known as Chinatown, has been settled by Chinese immigrants since the middle of the last century.

Where Dream and Reality Merge

In a city overflowing with attractions, business has to keep reaching out to potential customers . . .

In the dead of night and in my deep slumber a voice spoke without words: "Something has happened." I was asleep and I did not know whether it was joy or catastrophe that had overtaken me. Perhaps I was dead as so often happens in my dreams, perhaps I would wake on the other side of the grave. Opening my eyes I felt frightened. Then I remembered: this was not altogether the world of beyond. This was New York.

This was no mirage. New York was here, it was real.

Suddenly the truth burst on me through the deep blue sky, the soft, damp air. It was even more triumphant than the doubtful enchantments of the night before. It was nine o'clock on a Sunday morning, the streets were deserted, one or two neon signs still glowed. But there was not a person in sight, not a car in the street; nothing to break the rectilinear course of Eighth Avenue. Cubes, prisms, and parallelograms – the streets were concrete abstract designs, their surface looked like the abstract intersection made by two books; building materials had neither density nor texture; space itself had been poured into the moulds. I did not move. I looked. At last I was here, New York belonged to me. I felt again that joy I had known for fifteen years. I was leaving the station, and from the top of the monumental stairway I saw all the roofs of Marseilles spread out below me; I had a year, two years to pass alone in an unknown city; I did not move and I looked down, thinking: it is a strange town. It is my future and it will be my past. Between these houses that have existed for years without me are streets laid out for thousands of people to whom I do not, and never did, belong. But now I am walking, going down Broadway.

It's me all right. I walk in streets that were not built for me, and where my life has not yet left its tracks; here is no perfume of the past. No one knows of my presence; I am still a ghost, and I glide through the city without disturbing anyone. And yet henceforth my life would conform to the layout of the streets and houses; New York would belong to me, and I to it.

I drank an orange juice at a counter and sat down in a shoe-shiner's booth on one of three armchairs raised on a short flight of steps; little by little I came to life and grew accustomed to the city. The surfaces were now façades, the solids houses. In the roadway dust and old newspapers were drifting on the wind. After Washington Square all mathematics went by the

… here advertisers have taken their billboards to flat-topped house roofs.

board. Right angles are broken, streets are no longer numbered but named, lines get curved and confused. I was lost as though in some European town. The houses have only three or four floors, and deep colours varying between red, ochre and black; washing hangs out to dry on fire escapes that zig-zag up the buildings. Washing that promises sun, shoe-shine men posted at street corners, terraced roofs – they vaguely recall some southern town, and yet the faded red of the houses reminds one of London fogs. But this district does not resemble anything I know. I feel I shall love it.

Everything made me wonder; not only things unexpected but things I had foreseen. I did not know they had green canvas awnings outside the buildings in smart districts, bearing a large number, and advancing onto the pavement to denote some wedding, who knows? There was a porter on the threshold so that each house looked like an hotel or a bar. Also the entrance, guarded by uniformed commissionaires, was like the hall of a palace. The lift was worked by an employee: it is difficult to receive visitors in secret.

On the contrary, I had often seen these houses on the films without a porter and just like provincial houses at home. You go through the first glass door and you find a series of bells, one for each tenant; each has his letter-box. You ring and a second glass door opens. I also recognised the big flat push-bells I had seen in films, and their sound more muffled than that of our bells at home. What worried me was that these studio *décors* which I had never believed in should be so real.

So many small surprises in the course of the first few days gives them a peculiar charm. Nothing bored me. That business lunch in a restaurant on Fortieth Street was quite dismal; with its carpets, mirrors and chandeliers that place of elegance was like a tea shop in a big store, and of course it was too hot. But I was getting the flavour of America in my martini and my tomato juice; the meal was a kind of communion.

This charm is well worth while. But the exotic colour transfiguring each moment has its snares. It was a fine sunny day and I wanted to walk along the East river. But the drive, that wide, raised road which runs beside the river, is reserved for cars. I tried to cheat, and I advanced, hugging the wall. But it is difficult to cheat in America; everything works like a machine which serves you so long as you obey it; cars driven at sixty miles an hour along this *autostrada* brushed past me dangerously. There is a square beside the water, and people were walking there, but it seemed impossible to join them. I took

An explosion of light: Manhattan and Fifth Avenue at night.

courage and managed to reach the line that divides the traffic streams flowing in opposite directions, but I must stay there a long time, fixed like a street lamp, waiting for a sudden break in the traffic to gain the other side; and I still had to jump a railing before I was safe. Weighed down by my winter overcoat, too thick for the sunshine, I felt more tired than if I had climbed a mountain. A few minutes later I learnt that there are passages under the drive for pedestrians, and also bridges that cross it.

The river smelt of salt and spices. Men were sitting on benches in the sun: down-and-outs and negroes. Children on roller-skates shot across the asphalt, bumping into each other and shouting. In the edge of the drive they were building cheap apartment houses: these vast tapering buildings are ugly. But beyond them I could see the tall towers of the city and, across the river, Brooklyn. I sat down on a bench to the sound of roller-skates, I looked at Brooklyn and felt quite overwhelmed. So Brooklyn existed, Manhattan with its skyscrapers, and all America beyond the horizon; but I no longer existed. There it was. I knew what I was looking for: that sense of completeness that one knows only in childhood or in one's first youth when one becomes

altogether oblivious of oneself for something else. I had tasted this joy, this certitude, on other travels, but it was fugitive. Whether in Greece, in Italy, in Spain, in Africa, Paris remained for me the centre of the world; I had never quite left Paris; something of me was still there.

Now Paris had lost its power. Not only had I landed in a strange country, an autonomous country situated apart; but I had made contact with this world and it was here. It would be mine. But it would not only be mine; the evidence for its existence was too dazzling for me to take it in my net.

It would be a relevation experienced beyond the limits of my ordinary life. And suddenly I was free from the monotonous cares I call my life. I was but a charmed conscience to which the sovereign Object would soon reveal itself.

The noted French feminist, novelist and existentialist philosopher SIMONE DE BEAUVOIR visited the United States in 1947 on a nation-wide lecture tour, discussing the role of the female writer in the post-war era. The publication of her book America Day by Day, *labelled as anti-American by her critics, stimulated more controversy in America than her classic work* The Second Sex.

46

The Flat Iron Building, built in 1902, is famous for its three-cornered design resembling a giant clothes iron. This unusual style has saved it from the fate of many other buildings which have been demolished to make room for more profitable development.

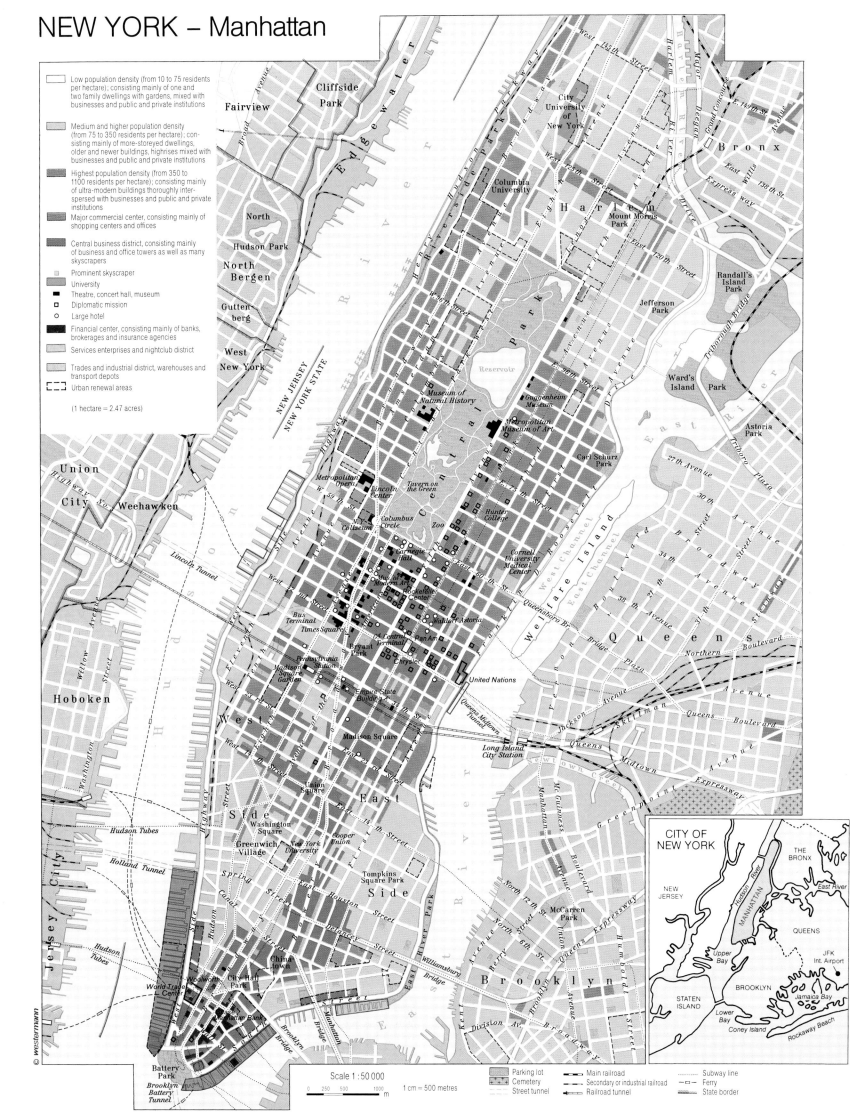

NEW YORK – Manhattan

Legend:

Low population density (from 10 to 75 residents per hectare); consisting mainly of one and two family dwellings with gardens, mixed with businesses and public and private institutions

Medium and higher population density (from 75 to 350 residents per hectare); consisting mainly of more-storeyed dwellings, older and newer buildings, highrises mixed with businesses and public and private institutions

Highest population density (from 350 to 1100 residents per hectare); consisting mainly of ultra-modern buildings thoroughly interspersed with businesses and public and private institutions

Major commercial center, consisting mainly of shopping centers and offices

Central business district, consisting mainly of business and office towers as well as many skyscrapers

- Prominent skyscraper
- University
- Theatre, concert hall, museum
- Diplomatic mission
- Large hotel

Financial center, consisting mainly of banks, brokerages and insurance agencies

Services enterprises and nightclub district

Trades and industrial district, warehouses and transport depots

Urban renewal areas

(1 hectare = 2.47 acres)

Scale 1 : 50 000

0   250   500   1000 m

1 cm = 500 metres

Parking lot
Cemetery
Street tunnel
Main railroad
Secondary or industrial railroad
Railroad tunnel
Subway line
Ferry
State border

© westermann

Labels on map:

Fairview, Cliffside Park, North Hudson Park, North Bergen, Guttenberg, West New York, Union City, Weehawken, Hoboken, Jersey City, New Jersey, New York State

Hudson River, Edgewater, Lincoln Tunnel, Holland Tunnel, Hudson Tubes, Brooklyn Battery Tunnel

Harlem, City University of New York, Columbia University, Mount Morris Park, Jefferson Park, Randall's Island Park, Ward's Island Park, Astoria Park, Bronx, Triborough Bridge, Triboro Plaza, Grand Concourse, Major Deegan Expressway, East Express way, Harlem River

Central Park, Reservoir, Museum of Natural History, Guggenheim Museum, Metropolitan Museum of Art, Carl Schurz Park, Tavern on the Green, Zoo, Metropolitan Opera, Lincoln Center, Coliseum, Columbus Circle, Hunter College, Cornell University Medical Center, Carnegie Hall, Mus. of Modern Art, Rockefeller Center, Bus Terminal, Times Square, Waldorf Astoria, Pan Am, Grand Central Terminal, Bryant Park, Chrysler, Pennsylvania Station, Madison Square Garden, Empire State Building, United Nations, Madison Square, Union Square, Washington Square, Greenwich Village, New York University, Cooper Union, Tompkins Square Park, East Side, West Side, China town, Woolworth, City Hall Park, World Trade Center, Chase Manhattan Bank, Battery Park

Roosevelt Island, Welfare Island, West Channel, East Channel, Queensboro Bridge, Queens Midtown Tunnel, Long Island City Station, Queens, Brooklyn, Newtown Creek, Greenpoint, McCarren Park, Williamsburg Bridge, Manhattan Bridge, Brooklyn Bridge, East River, Northern Boulevard, Queens Boulevard, Jackson Avenue, Skillman Avenue, Greenpoint Expressway

Inset:

CITY OF NEW YORK

NEW JERSEY, Hudson River, MANHATTAN, THE BRONX, East River, QUEENS, Upper Bay, BROOKLYN, STATEN ISLAND, Lower Bay, Jamaica Bay, Coney Island, Rockaway Beach, JFK Int. Airport

CONTENTS

GENERAL FACTS

DISTRICTS. New York is divided into five administrative areas, or boroughs: Brooklyn, The Bronx, Manhattan, Queens and Staten Island. The largest of these is Brooklyn, with four million residents. Manhattan is the most frequently visited of the boroughs, and also the smallest.

ETHNIC QUARTERS. As a result of New York's historic development, the city is a conglomeration of ethnically distinct quarters where people are much more conscious of their different origins than most Americans living elsewhere. Many people prefer to live in "their" territorys; some quarters occupy less room than half a street block, while others such as Chinatown are an entire suburb. You can get an impression of New York's ethnic variety from the following – incomplete – list: Manhattan: Chinese (Chinatown: south of Canal Street); Italian (Little Italy: Mulberry Street and its side streets); Jewish (Essex Street and a wide part of the Lower East Side); Ukrainian (East 6th Street, Lexington Avenue in the 30s streets); Irish (Inwood: the north end of Manhattan); Cuban/Spanish (14th Street and 8th Avenue). Brooklyn: Lebanese (Atlantic Avenue); Russian (Brighton Beach); Chadian Jews (Williamsburg); Italian/ Irish/Scandinavian (Bay Ridge). Queens: Greek (Astoria); Latin American (Jackson Heights and Elmhurst).

The Statue of Liberty in New York Harbour.

POPULATION. Eight million people live in New York. Just over half (52 percent) are White but their numbers are dwindling. The population includes two million Jews, one million Italians, 100,000 Greeks and 100,000 Chinese. Almost one-quarter (24 percent) of New Yorkers are black, while 20 percent are Hispanic (including 1.64 million Puerto Ricans). The remaining four percent are mostly Asian, including Koreans, Japanese, Vietnamese, Taiwanese and East Indians. The Asian population continues to grow (6 percent in the last 10 years).

The average annual income of a white New York household is about 16,000 dollars; the average black household income is only 11,000 dollars. The official poverty line for a familiy of four living in New York is 12,675 dollars. The number of people in New York living on social welfare – approximately 800,000 – equals the size of the eleventh largest city in the United States. There are some 60,000 homeless people in New York, but an equal number of millionaires.

POSITION. New York is situated on the same latitude as Naples (42 degrees north) and 73 degrees west longitude in the mouth of the Hudson River on the Atlantic Ocean.

WEATHER

New York's weather is really pleasant only during the few weeks prior to the start of summer and then again in late summer. For the rest of the year, it is either a hot and humid sub-tropical climate or else wet and cold. The average day-time high temperatures are 4°C (40°F) in January, 16°C (59°F) in April, and 29°C (86°F) in July. Average lows are –3°C (30°F) in January, 7°C (46°F) in April, 20°C (68°F) in July, and 11°C (52°F) in October.

NEW YORK ABBREVIATIONS

It is useful to know some of the abbreviations which appear in New York's newspapers and conversations:

BBQs: apart from meaning barbecue, this is a disparaging reference to the residents of Brooklyn, The Bronx and Queens.

B & Ts: Bridge and Tunnel people – weekend visitors to Manhattan Island from other parts of New York and beyond who travel via bridges the island's bridges and tunnels.

BMT: an underground train line.

BQE: the Brooklyn-Queens Expressway.

CoOp: an apartment owned by the occupant.

C. U. N.Y.: City University of New York.

FDR: Franklin Delano Roosevelt; the name of an expressway on the East River.

HBO: Home Box Office, a cable TV channel specialising in cinema films.

IND/IRT: underground train lines.

IRS: Internal Revenue Service, or taxation department.

JFK: John F. Kennedy Airport.

LIE: Long Island Expressway.

LIRR: Long Island Railroad, the suburban train service connecting with the island.

MTA: Metropolitan Transit Authority.

NYU: New York University, situated in Greenwich Village.

OTB: Off Track Betting, horse racing betting offices.

PATH: trains run by the New York Port Authority connecting New York with New Jersey.

PBS: Public Broadcasting Service, a government-funded television channel (Channel 13).

SI: Staten Island.

TKTS: kiosks where reduced price theatre tickets can be bought.

VD: veneral disease.

WASP: White Anglo-Saxon Protestant, the description of a certain category of East Coast resident; also used to identity a member of the so-called ruling political/business establishment.

ARRIVAL AND ORIENTATION

John F. Kennedy Airport is for most visitors the door to the new world. Carey Company buses provide a link between the airport terminals and the city every 20 or 30 minutes. It is a 45-minute ride to Manhattan's Park Avenue Bus Station, opposite Grand Central Railway Station and the location of a number of big hotels. Carey buses also serve New York's other airports.

City council-owned buses of the Q-10 line commute between the airport terminals and the subway stations of Lefferts Boulevard and Kew Gardens, from where you can continue via lines A, F, and E. Taxis take just as long to reach the city as the buses.

Orientation in Manhatten is reasonably easy because of the quadrangular layout of the streets. The avenues run north-south and are numbered just like the streets running east-west. The numbering system of the avenues goes from east to west. For the streets, the numbering begins north of Houston Street.

Nevertheless, there is some confusion because south of Houston Street, the streets can also have names, and in certain sections, avenues are also named. For example, Seventh Avenue in the area of streets numbered in the thirties is also called Fashion Avenue. And Sixth Avenue is officially known as the called Avenue of the Americas, but most New Yorkers still call it Sixth Avenue. In Harlem, all the avenues west of Fifth Avenue are given names.

House numbers are also dependent on their east-west position: all house numbers east of Fifth Avenue begin with an "E" while all those west of the Avenue take a "W". The lower the house number, the closer it will be to Fifth Avenue. You can reach a New York address quickest when the nearest street junction is also known.

you must have the correct money, or an underground train token. There are two bus stations: the largest, on 42nd Street/Eighth Avenue, serves the west and south; the smaller one, on 181st Street, serves the north and northeast.

RAILWAY STATIONS. There are two: Grand Central Station on 42nd Street/Park Avenue and Pennsylvania Station on 34th Street/Seventh Avenue. Trains stop at only one or the other of the stations; there are no rail connections between the two.

TRANSPORT

AIRPORTS. New York has three airports: John F. Kennedy in Brooklyn, La Guardia in Queens and Newark in New Jersey. All three can be easily reached by bus and train, and are connected with one another by a bus system.

BUSES. City council buses serve the avenues, operating services uptown or downtown along the streets, i.e., from east to west and back. At each bus stop you will find a route plan. The buses, like the subway trains, operate around the clock.

A transfer ticket, bought from the driver, allows you to make one change per journey. Drivers don't give change, so

THE SUBWAY. The New York subway offers the quickest and the cheapest form of transportion in the city. For one dollar, you can buy a token valid for a whole day of travel on the entire one-hundred-fifty-six mile/two-hundred-fifty kilometre network. Tokens can be bought at kiosks in subway stations. The dangers of using the subway are known worldwide. The fact is, however, that about four-and-a-half million passengers use the system daily without thinking about the chances of being attacked. You are more likely to arrive safely at your destination if you know which way you need to travel. Over the entrance to each station there is a plan showing the main routes, either uptown or downtown, to Brooklyn or The Bronx. A map of the subway

Always on the move: New York taxis on 42nd Street/Fifth Avenue.

network offers invaluable help and free copies can be obtained wherever you buy tokens. The map also identifies those connecting stations where only passengers travelling in a certain direction can get off.

Connecting stations also have coloured map guides to assist you on your way; occasionally, it is necessary to walk several hundred yards along the underground tunnel paths. Trains are less frequent at night, which means longer waiting times on station platforms. If you choose to travel by subway at night, for

New York's quickest and cheapest transportation: the subway.

your own safety you should wait in the designated Off Hour Waiting Areas marked out in yellow until your train arrives. Then get into one of the middle carriages where the conductor is based.

TAXIS. Many taxis in New York are not equipped with radios but they seem to roll endlessly along the streets and will stop to pick up passengers anywhere. It's a good system: you simply stand on the curb and hail a passing "cab" which has the free for hire sign lit up on the roof; ideally, the taxi will be headed in the direction you want to travel. The metered fare is $1.50 for the first ninth of a mile and thereafter 10 cents for every tenth of a mile. Note: if you should end up in the area south of Houston Street, you may

need to show the cabbie the way yourself!

GENERAL INFORMATION

The most useful source of information about cultural and other events, as well as details about shopping, are the local pages of the New York Times newspaper and in particular the Weekend Guide section which is published every Friday. The Sunday edition of the newspaper – which is so big it weighs more than two pounds/one kilogram – lists what's on in the cinemas, theatres, art and photo galleries and museums. The weekly Village Voice newspaper is also an invaluable source of the types of information too complicated for a travel guide to include. The Voice carries informative advertisements for restaurants and clubs as well as providing critical journalistic coverage of local politics. The illustrated weekly New York Magazine reports on topical events in the city and includes a list of useful addresses.

The New York Convention and Visitor's Bureau at Columbus Circle is an important starting place for tourists. The Bureau offers brochures on sightseing, city maps, details of events, free studio audience tickets for television shows, reduced price tickets for Broadway

performances, and advice on budget-priced hotels. The Bureau also has a branch office on the south side of Times Square. If you would like to find out more about the city's history, architecture, literature, ethnic composition, museums, nightlife or restaurants, visit the New York Bookstore (43 West 54th Street) and see what they have on offer. All types of businesses and services are listed in the Yellow Pages of the telephone book.

TELECOMMUNICATIONS

THE POST. The post network is confined to handling letters and parcels. There is a post office in every suburb and the addresses are listed in the telephone book under United States Postal Service. Manhattan's two main post offices are on 33rd Street/Eighth Avenue and Lexington Avenue/45th Street. Both are open on Sundays from 11am to 3pm. Telegrams are handled by private firms such as Western Union and Federal Express, both of which also offer an express letter delivery service.

USING THE TELEPHONE. New York City has two area codes – 212 for Manhattan and The Bronx, 718 for Brooklyn, Queens and Staten Island. If you want to telephone from Manhattan to Brooklyn, for example, you first dial 1, then the area code 718, followed by the private number. A local call from a telephone booth costs twenty-five cents for eight minutes; insert the money first and then dial. After eight minutes the operator will interrupt and advise you to insert more money if you wish to continue your call. For long distance calls, deposit twenty-five cents to reach the Operator who will then tell you how much more you need to insert for a three-minute call. You will be connected to the number only after having inserted the full amount. It is also possible to make a collect call whereby the receiver of your call pays the bill. Contact the Operator who then calls the person with whom you wish to speak to find out if they will accept the charge for your call. Public telephones also accept incoming calls.

LOCAL CUSTOMS AND TIPPING

New Yorkers are very casual people and you can find yourself on first name terms with even passing acquaintances. But politeness is nonetheless important. If you accidentally bump into someone on a bus or train it is proper to say: "Excuse me, please". When you arrive at a restaurant you should wait to be shown to a table by a waiter or waitress; it is considered rude to simply select your own table.

Service personnel expect a tip of at least 15 percent. Restaurant bills include the 8.5 percent sales tax. Taxi drivers also expect a tip of 15 percent.

SAFETY PRECAUTIONS

The United States is known for its high level of crime, and in New York violence is a part of everyday life. Given that fact, it is a good idea to listen to advice from friends or acquaintances warning you of visiting certain districts or quarters. Nevertheless, virtually all parts of New York can be visited, including some notorious quarters: it is a question of using common sense to decide where and when you go. There is no reason for a visitor to avoid, for example, the Studio Museum in Harlem, or the famous La Marqueta street market in Spanish Harlem. However, the visitor who is naive enough to wander into run-down ghettos to take pictures of burned-out houses for his slide show back home can hardly expect sympathy if the residents react unfavourably. The following rules should be observed:

• Never venture into parks at night except for example, when concerts are being held in Central Park
• Never carry more money than you need for the day or evening. Traveller's cheques and credit cards are safer than cash.
• Avoid looking like a typical tourist. Handbags, cameras, new clothes and other signs of newness act like a magnet in some districts. Keep a close watch on your belongings in the underground; do not put bags on the ground and avoid waiting near doors.
• Plan your routes. If you have to use dark streets to reach home, try to travel through crowded locations. Many small shops and bars stay open late and offer some security.
• If you are attacked it is advisable to give up your money and valuables rather than putting up resistance.

ACCOMMODATION

Hotel rooms are generally expensive and breakfast is not usually included. The most expensive hotels are situated on the southern edge of Central Park and on Park Avenue; the cheapest are in the area of Pennsylvania Railway Station (34th Street/Seventh Avenue). Many hotels have reduced weekend rates and it is worth asking about these. If you are on a tight budget try the YMCA, which offers not only economic rooms but also laundering facilities and some tourist information. General information on accommodation is available at the New York Convention and Visitor's Bureau at Columbus Circle; hotels are listed in the Yellow Pages telephone book.

FOOD AND DRINK

ALCOHOLIC DRINKS. All alcohol, with the exception of beer, is sold exclusively in state-licensed stores, which are closed on Sundays. Beer can be bought in supermarkets, delis and other shops around the clock.

BARS. There are thousands to choose from, in every style and price range. Most Irish-managed bars serve draught beer, which does not taste as insipid as beer sold in the bottle or can. The American contribution to the international drinking scene has more to do with the invention of fantastic cocktails than the art of brewing. Every barman from the Upper East and West Sides to SoHo and Midtown can mix a Long Island Ice Tea or a Screwdriver. Their customers are yuppies, artists and night owls. But whether you sit at a table or lean on the bar, you will be expected to pay a 15 percent tip per drink. So if you plan to have more than one drink expect to see the dollars in your pocket disappear.

DELICATESSENS ("DELIS"). These small shops, catering to the different ethnic communities, are often open late and always have on sale crisp fresh fruit and vegetables, as well as a rich selection of salad items.

RESTAURANTS. The best place to head for culinary delights are the ethnic quarters of New York, particularly Chinatown and Little Italy in Manhattan where there are numerous excellent venues. For those in search of more unusual tastes, head beyond Manhattan into Brooklyn, Queens and The Bronx. Here you will find Lebanese, Korean, Arabian, Scandinavian and – in Brighton Beach, with its ocean views – Russian food. In the City Island area of The Bronx and the Sheepshead Bay area of Brooklyn you will find restaurants serving fresh seafood. Greenwich Village offers a broad choice of good restaurants, including places catering especially to vegetarians. If you do not want to rely on restaurant guides, most of which are out-of-date by

A distinguished address: the Plaza Hotel on Fifty-Ninth Street in the heart of New York City.

the time they are published, take note of the restaurant test reports in the New York Times. The Village Voice also regularly tests different restaurants. (For further information see LOCAL CUSTOMS AND TIPPING and GENERAL INFORMATION).

SNACKS. The most popular fast food in New York is the hot dog, also known as a frankfurter or simply a frank; you can find a mobile snackbar on almost every street corner selling them. They usually come served with fried onions and tomato ketchup or mustard. The second most beloved street snack is the knish, a type of potato pastry or pancake, but they can sometimes taste like wet cardboard.

SHOPPING

You can buy almost anything in New York at night as well as during the day. You can find out about many special offers by reading through the daily newspapers, in particular the New York Post and the Daily News, as well as the weekly magazines. Special supplements in the New York Times, for example the science supplement on Wednesdays, carry advertisements for computer shops. On Sundays, there is a supplement on camera equipment and videos. The New York Magazine carries a special offers column. Many sales last only one day, some only a matter of a few hours.

In Manhattan, there are whole streets, even entire districts, of shops specialising

Above: Sausages on Sixth Avenue. Below: Bread in the East Village.

A delicatessen ("deli") and salad bar.

in certain products or services. On 47th Street you will find jewellers and diamond traders; in and around 32nd Street there are camera equipment shops; along Seventh Avenue in the area of the thirty streets are fashion shops; and between Astor Place and Canal Street on Broadway there are second-hand shops. On Sundays there is a big clothing market along Orchard Street in the Jewish part of the Lower East Side. A rich selection of musical instruments can be found on 48th Street in the area of Sixth Avenue. Anyone who likes haggling over prices should head for 14th and 34th Streets in search of stereo and video equipment and cameras, but you need to have a good idea of the market and the product you are looking for if you don't want to risk being taken. Expect to pay the sales tax of 8.5 percent on all goods.

FESTIVALS

There is always something to celebrate in New York. It could be one of the official days of the big immigrant communities such as St. Patrick's Day in March (Irish) and San Gennaro in September (Italian), the traditionally colourful parades on Fifth Avenue, or one of the numerous street, house or block parties held during summer weekends in the ethnic quarters. These parties are more interesting than the big Fifth Avenue parades because they offer a variety of music, food and drink and the chance to meet people.

The dates and locations of the street parties can be found in the Weekend Guide of the Friday edition of the New York Times and the events section of the Village Voice.

Other traditional festivals in New York include: **Chinese New Year**, 21 January – 19 February; **Easter Parade** on Fifth Avenue; **Food Market** (mid-May) on 9th Avenue, with food stalls stretching for twenty street blocks; **Annual Gay Pride Week** (last week of June), which includes a colourful parade; **JVC Jazz Festival** (in June); **the Museums Mile Celebration** (also June); **Mostly Mozart** (July), a series of concerts by the New York Philharmonic Orchestra in the Lincoln Center; **Washington Square Park Music Festival** (July); Joseph Papp's performances of **Shakespeare** in Central Park (July); **Harlem Day** (last week of August); **San Gennaro's Day**

(September), when the whole of Little Italy is out on the streets dancing; **New York Marathon** (last week of October); **Columbus Day; Hallowe'en Parade;** and in the last hours of the year, the **New Year's Eve** celebrations in Times Square.

CULTURE AND ENTERTAINMENT

ART GALLERIES. They are scattered throughout New York, even in Brooklyn and The Bronx, but three districts are located in Manhattan. Those on **57th Street** cater to a conservative type of customer in search of pictures of both a high quality and guaranteed value appreciation. The big galleries in **SoHo**, particularly on West Broadway and its surrounding side streets, offer modern and fashionable art. The third art quarter is in **East Village** on the Lower East Side, where many struggling artists live and work. Galleries here will risk dealing with unknown painters and experimental styles. Apart from the art galleries, there are a large number of photographic galleries. Addresses and details of exhibitions are listed in the Sunday supplements of the New York Times and events calendars of the Village Voice.

Above: The Hard Rock Cafe. Below: The "Old Fashioned Pub" on 43rd Street/Broadway.

CLUBS. A large slice of social life, particularly among single people, is to be found in the clubs. They are not places simply to buy an expensive drink and listen to loud music. New York clubs are more: they are galleries, theatre halls, and party cellars all in one. The provide an impression of the New York lifestyle, a window on the city's night life. In order to remain attractive to the easily bored New Yorkers, many clubs are redecorated every couple of months. Most clubs are to be found Downtown, south of 23rd Street, in East Village, SoHo, Tribeca and Greenwich Village. For a more detailed guide to the club scene, read the advertisements on the back pages of the Village Voice. It is unusual to visit a club before midnight.

MUSEUMS. New York's museums are a major attraction, with the centrepiece being the world famous **Museum of Modern Art** and its three floors of international exhibits covering the 20th Century. The reputation of the "MoMa," as the museum is nicknamed, rests on its extensive design and photography departments, and its regular special subject exhibitions.

The **Metropolitan Museum of Art** has a collection of antiquities, but above all, in the Rockefeller Wing, a splendid collection of primitive African art. The circular-shaped **Guggenheim Museum** shows European classics of the modern style, while the **Whitney Museum** concentrates on contemporary American painting. The Whitney always draws special attention through its video projects. At the classical building of the United States' fourth largest art museum, the **Brooklyn Museum**, you will find an interesting Egyptian collection.

Other interesting museums include the **Museum of Natural History** offering hours of fun and excitement for children (the giant nature cinema has a 360 degree screen); the **Museum of Broadcasting**, plotting the history of American television; the **Museum of the City of New York**; the **Museum of Immigration** on Ellis Island, telling the story of the daily processing of the thousands of immigrants who first set foot in the United States in its halls; the story of New York as a port is traced at the **South Street Seaport Museum**, which also has attractively-priced restaurants and bars. Also worthwhile seeing are the **Studio Museum of Harlem** (past and present history of Afro-Americans); the **Museo del Barrio** (history of the Puerto Rican immigrants); **Museum of the American Indian** (art and artifacts). Finally, New York has a floating military museum, aboard the Second World War aircraft carrier **Intrepid** (Pier 86, West 42nd Street).

Beyond those listed above, there are numerous small museums often overlooked by visitors but well worth seeing. They include a fire brigade museum, a museum of holography, an anatomy museum, a film museum and a children's museum. Full lists of the changing exhibitions and programmes in art and other museums are published in the New York Times, the Village Voice, the New York Magazine and the New Yorker.

MUSIC. With virtually all the country's big music companies based here, music is a major New York export. Perhaps less known is the fact that New York is the centre of production for salsa and is the world capital of jazz. Visitors to New York have an inexhaustible choice of live

Above: Trend-setters or original style. Below: Antiques for sale on Sixth Avenue.

Above: Manhattan skyscrapers. Below: The Metropolitan Museum of Art.

these smaller venues, among which can be recommended Joseph Papp's Public Theatre on Astor Place and, representing the off-off scene, La Mama on East 4th Street. The Black theatre scene should also be investigated, as well as the many companies of the other ethnic and social minorities. A good assessment of the theatre scene can be found in the Village Voice and the features pages of the New York Times.

SIGHTSEEING

Numbers in italics refer to colour photographs.

ARCHITECTURE. There is a little of everything representing Europe's entire architectural history to be seen in Manhattan, from ancient Greek temples to ecclesiastical Gothic and the ultra-modern skyscraper. Of course, the "historic" buildings are mostly fakes, like the famous St. Patrick's Cathedral on Fifth Avenue which resembles the Cologne Cathedral in Germany.

Typical New York architecture is to be found in the brownstones – usually two or three storey red-brown brick houses with a short flight of steps leading up to a narrow hall. Living rooms are mainly at the front, with the kitchen and bedrooms at the rear. Also typical of this type of building are the sash windows, tarred flat roofs, and fire escapes on the outside walls featured in so many New York films. Brownstone houses are usually terraced, in the style of London's town houses of the eighteenth and nineteenth centuries. You can see brownstones, in **Greenwich Village**, **East Village**, **Chelsea**, **Brooklyn Heights** and – faith-fully reconstructed in the original style, on **Stuyvesant Street** and **Schermer-horn Row** in south Manhattan.

A slice of American architectural history can also be seen in the galleries and fashion district of **SoHo** south of Houston Street (SoHo is the abbreviation for **South of Houston**). This is where some of North America's earliest cast-iron superstructures, forerunners to today's highrise buildings, can be found. Cast-iron structures first appeared in the second half on the last century, chiefly in the building of factories and warehouses. In SoHo today, some of these buildings are decorated with façades of Greek Doric

music, ranging from the Metropolitan Opera and the other temple of classical music – the Lincoln Center – to numerous jazz haunts or rock clubs. But if you want to save the admission price, head for the streets of Manhattan where you are certain to encounter a variety of street musicians every day of the week. Details of concerts and bar and club music can be found in the Village Voice and the Friday edition of the New York Times.

THEATRE. No other city in the world offers as much theatre as New York where there is a daily choice of almost two

hundred productions. The choice ranges from the big air-conditioned, computer-operated halls on Broadway to the small stages of the off-off scene.

There are only a couple of dozen theatres on Broadway, in and around Times Square, where the big budget productions – mostly musicals – of New York's extravagant theatre world are performed. The heavier theatre scene is to be found on the smaller stages off Broadway, catering to audiences of between one hundred and five hundred persons, scattered across Manhattan and parts of Brooklyn. The real vitality and variety of New York's theatre life is to be found in

pillars and are now home to galleries, upmarket boutiques and souvenir shops. But it is the skyscrapers for which New York is most reknown. The classic ones include the neo-Gothic **Woolworth Building** (Broadway/corner of City Hall), designed as a vertical version of London's parliament building *(34/35)*; the three-cornered **Flat Iron Building** (23rd Street/corner of Broadway) *(47)*, and the Art Deco **Chrysler Building** with its steel top (Lexington Avenue/corner of 51st Street). Apart from enjoying the overall design of the Chrysler Building, it is well worth taking a look inside at some of the small details, for example the letter boxes, the doors of the lift and the ceiling paintings. One of the landmarks of New York, however, is the **Empire State Building** *(2)* on Fifth Avenue/32nd Street. Built between 1929 and 1931, the Empire State was for decades the tallest building in the world. Standing on the Art Deco viewing platform on a clear day, it is possible to see for about sixty miles/one hundred kilometres. The top of the twin-towered **World Trade Center** *(34/ 35)* is also open to the public.

In the 1960s and 1970s, architectural style mostly moved indoors. Monumental works of art and even gardens were planted in the large fashionable entrance halls. For example, in the **Ford Foundation Building** (320 East 43rd Street) the architects fashioned a display of granite and greenery costing sixteen million dollars. Architects for the computer giant **IBM** countered with a building (53rd Avenue/Madison Avenue) which included a bamboo garden and art gallery, while the entrance hall of **Trump Tower** (Fifth Avenue/53rd Street) boasts a seventy-four-foot/twenty-three-metre high waterfall over pink granite, which in the eyes of many critics crosses the boundary of good taste to become pure kitsch.

ART. In addition to New York's museums and galleries, attentive art enthusiasts will want to take a look at New York's outdoor artistic attractions. Some examples include: Jean Dubuffet's monumental sculpture called "Five Trees", on the Chase Manhattan Bank Plaza in the banking district; Pablo Picasso's equally monumental "Portrait Sylvette" in University Village (near Washington Square Park); and Isamo Noguchi's red "Cube" in front of the

Above: The Empire State Building. Below: In Central Park.

Midland Building on Lower Broadway. Nearby, in the small Nevelson Plaza Park, you can see seven large sculptures by Louise Nevelson (Maiden Street, corner of William Street). During summer, one of the city council-supported cultural groups places art works in different parts of the city – often in locations where both visitors and New Yorkers would least expect to find them.

BEACHES. Why not visit a beach in New York? Altogether, there are fifteen miles/twenty-five kilometres of sandy beaches, all of which are quickly reached by subway.

The most famous is **Coney Island** in Brooklyn, where on hot summer weekends up to half a million people will bake in the sun. With its mile-long promenade (the boardwalk) and Astroland Fun Park, Coney Island is always worth a visit (reached by subway lines F, M, N, Q) and has remained a favourite tourist attraction. A little farther east, **Brighton Beach** is less hectic and has the added attraction of Russian beach bars. In The Bronx, **Orchard Beach** offers quiet still water and a pretty surrounding landscape (reached by subway line 6 to the terminus station Pelham Park, then by bus BX12).

The Brooklyn Bridge.

The cleanest beaches are at **Rockaway Beach**, which is washed by the Atlantic tide (reached by subway lines A and C). But prettier, wider, cleaner and quieter beaches are to be found on Long Island – **Jones Beach**, **Long Beach**, or the beaches on **Fire Island**, popular with the gay community.

These beaches are reminiscent of the French Atlantic coast (reached by the LIRR suburban railway, telephone 1-718-739-4200 for details).

BRIDGES. Nineteen bridges link Manhattan with New York's other boroughs, but the most attractive and famous is the **Brooklyn Bridge**. The neo-Gothic suspension bridge connects the financial district with Brooklyn over the East River, and is part of the world reknown breathtaking view of the Manhattan skyline and New York Bay. The truss-like construction of **Manhattan Bridge** along with the gently swinging **Williamsburg Bridge** are impressive for their harmonious elegance. Both bridges also connect Manhattan and Brooklyn but cannot be crossed on foot. At the north end of Manhattan, spanning the Hudson

River, **George Washington Bridge** offers a magnificent view of Manhattan.

BROOKLYN HEIGHTS/WATERFRONT. Civic pride and a zest for the European way of life radiates out of Brooklyn Heights, a favourite district of the wealthy and intellectuals not living in Manhattan. Thomas Wolfe, John Dos Passos, Truman Capote, Norman Mailer and many other writers lived and worked here. Film makers always treat the district with respect.

The sidewalk cafés, shops and restaurants of Montague and Pierremont Streets merge into a promenade – The Esplanade – which gives a marvellous panorama of south Manhattan and New York Bay.

Underneath Brooklyn Bridge is the gourmet restaurant and bar "River Cafe". In the immediate neighbourhood – scattered around the Jehova Witness society's complex – there are numerous Italian restaurants with a Neopolitan atmosphere.

CENTRAL PARK. This park in the heart of Manhattan is more than just a green lung for the city: it is an architectural masterpiece also providing almost unlimited outdoor attractions and

facilities. Central Park is an exercise area for joggers and cyclists, a haven of peace and contemplation, with a sports ground, swimming pool, zoo, bird protection zone, children's playground, and a venue for open-air concerts. The best time to see Central Park is on Sundays in the summer, when it becomes a peaceful rendezvous for the city's numerous cultures. During the summer there are numerous outdoor classical concerts, as well as the Joseph Papp Shakespeare performances.

Whenever the New York Philharmonic Orchestra gives a performance, up to two-hundred-thousand music lovers turn out with their picnic baskets and blankets. Pop concerts featuring world famous performers will attract audiences of half-a-million to the "big meadow." You can explore Central Park by horse-drawn buggy, hired on 59th Street at the southern edge of the park. 4/5

CHINATOWN. A great crush of swirling humanity and a thousand exotic smells greet the visitor to the tiny streets and alleys south of Canal Street where about 100,000 Chinese live in rather cramped conditions. Despite the expansion of Chinatown – to Little Italy and the Jewish Lower East Side – **Mott Street** remains the centre of the Chinese community. Alongside the numerous shops with their countless offers of Chinese goods, the majority of New York's restaurants, offering a choice of cuisine from the different regions of China are to be found here.

The least touristy area of Chinatown but nonetheless just as attractive is east of the Bowery. **East Broadway** is home to the Chinese printers, offices and insurance agents, next to Jewish and Latin American businesses. **Catherine Street** is the home of the Chinese animal market: living and dead pigs and pigeons mingle in shop windows alongside exotic vegetables.

CIRCLE LINE. The boat tour circling Manhattan lasts about three hours.

Between April and November, the boats depart daily beginning at 9.30 am from Pier 83 at the end of West 43rd Street.

EAST VILLAGE. The centre of the Downtown scene – home in particular to painters, musicians, those who live on their wits and, recently, yuppies – is around **St. Mark's Place, Third Avenue** and **Tompkins Square.** But in between the second-hand boutiques, sushi bars, and record shops, it is still possible to find traces of the old East Village: Polish, Ukrainian and Indian restaurants, an Orthodox church, eccentric shops, avant garde artists and more shifty types. On weekends, East Village is the focal point of the Bridge and Tunnel People as well as other visitors to Manhattan.

FIFTH AVENUE. New York's prestigious homes and shops are to be found chiefly in the area of streets numbered in the fifties. These streets, as well as the **Rockefeller Center,** form the most glitzy, exclusive, visited and photographed area of Manhattan. This is where you will find elegant shops and stores such as Saks, Lord & Taylor's, Altman's and Tiffany's. The so-called **Museums Mile** is between the 80th and 100th Streets, where Fifth Avenue borders Central Park. The museums here include the Museo del Barrio (105th Street), the Museum of the City of New York (103rd – 105th Streets), the Metropolitan Museum of Art (82nd Street), the International Center of Photography (94th Street) and the Guggenheim Museum (89th Street).

44/45

Above and middle: Businesses in Chinatown. Bottom: Tobacco shops on Seventh Avenue.

Above: Sex shop on 42nd Street. Below: Black street musician in Times Square.

FORTY-SECOND STREET (42nd Street). This legendary street – once the subject of a musical – is a mixture of the grand and the dingy. In the area of the **United Nations Quarter**, the **Grand Hyatt Hotel** and **Grand Central Station** *(26)*, 42nd Street is framed by noble buildings; around the **Public Library of New York** *(18)* it is relatively peaceful. But from **Times Square** *(25)* down to the Hudson River, the street is gloomy and unpleasant. When people talk about the "shadowy side of the city jungle", they could be referring to this end of 42nd Street, with its pornographic cinemas, drug handling and prostitution.

The excesses in the area of Times Square may be offensive, but at the same time the shabbiness is also typical of New York. However, some people – investors prominent among them – want to carry out a big renovation programme to shake up the area. The first steps along this road have already been taken; on the west side of 42nd Street around Times Square, new theatres and hotels have been built.

GREENWICH VILLAGE/THE WEST VILLAGE. This area is typical of New York: a restless tourist ghetto, centre of homosexuality, university campus, with elegant homes in the style of a small

Dutch town. Night or day, the best place to begin a tour is **Washington Square Park**. A mixture of people – students, street musicians, marijuana dealers as well as pensioners playing chess – meet here in the shadow of the **Triumph Arch**. Policemen wearing bored expressions stroll through the crowds on their daily patrols. Along the nearby **Bleecker** and **Eighth Streets**, as well as the entire area west of **Seventh Avenue**, there are enticing restaurants of all types, clubs, bars, boutiques, in addition to record, shoe and souvenir shops. Particularly worth seeing is **Jefferson Market Library**, built in a neo-Victorian style reminiscent of a fairy tale castle (Sixth Avenue/Tenth Street).

Homosexuals around the world know **Christopher Street** and its surrounding side streets as an east coast equivalent to the western San Francisco. There are homosexual theatres, cinemas, sports groups and – along with other cultural initiatives of New York's Gay community – a men's choir. The district also boasts a rich choice of restaurants, cafés and leather shops, but above all a string of bars stretching to the piers of the Hudson River.

HARLEM. Even though only five percent of New York's black population lives in Harlem, the suburb north of Central Park is recognised as the *black capital of the country*. Harlem is a suburb with a Janus-face: on one side a disreputable ghetto, on the other a living expression of a tradition-rich culture.

Most tourists prefer to visit Harlem on one of the numerous bus sightseeing tours of New York (details from the Convention and Visitors' Bureau). But the individual tourist can wander about the following districts of Harlem without too much concern: the centre around **125th Street**; the area of **Schomburg Library**, the largest library documenting black culture (515 Lenox Avenue); western Harlem in the streets around **City College** (where Robert Kennedy studied); and **Sugar Hill**, the residential locality of middle class blacks (140th – 155th Streets).

Places particularly worthwhile visiting are the **Apollo Theatre** (253 West 125th Street), for more than half a century a centre of black cultural entertainment; the elegant homes on **Lenox Terrace** (West 135th Street between Lenox and Fifth

Times Square: The famous, but now demolished, neon façade.

corner of the world, with consequently high levels of social problems such as disease, child mortality and crime. There are still traces of the district's former prominence as a trading port. "Boozer's Alley" or the **Bowery** (Third Avenue) is a surviving reminder of this past.

Today, the largest ethnic minorities are the Puerto Ricans (south of Houston Street), Jews (Essex Street and adjoining streets), Chinese (in the Canal Street locality), Poles and Ukrainians (East Village); the area is also home to many artists and tourists. All visitors should see the Jewish bakeries and cake shops south of Houston Street; the individual and cultural jumble of **East Village**; the privately-run **Amato Opera** on the Bowery; the cast-iron colonnades on **Lafayette Street** (near Astor Place); Joseph Papp's **Public Theatre** (Lafayette Street); and the flea markets operating around the clock on **Astor Place**.

MARKETS. Markets are a New York tradition which have resisted the pressures of modernisation. Apart from permanent markets such as **La Marqueta** (see Harlem), the kosher food stands on **Essex Street**, and the Chinese stalls of **Canal** and **Mulberry Streets**, there are also many weekly food markets selling fresh produce from the countryside. Flea markets are another beloved institution. Two of the best can be found on the west part of **Canal Street** and on **Essex Street** (corner with Delancey Street). On Sundays, many car parks become flea markets. The colourful **Chelsea Flower Market** is on Sixth Avenue (between 26th and 29th Streets). The palms and other greenery assembled on the pavement resemble a jungle path.

PROSPECT PARK/PARK SLOPE. Prospect Park in the heart of Brooklyn has less hustle and bustle and more peace and quiet than the larger Central Park. Both parks were designed by the same team.

Prospect Park's chief attractions are the **Botanical Gardens** and the **Japanese Garden**. The Ryoanji Temple rock garden is a replica from Kyoto, a place of harmony and contemplation which is rare in New York.

Adjacent is the Roji Garden with a Japanese teahouse atmosphere. Close by is the **Brooklyn Museum**, noted around the world for its Egyptian collection.

Avenue); and the lovingly tended townhouses in **Striver's Row** (West 138th Street). The famous street market **La Marqueta** in East Harlem, more typical of Latin America than Manhattan, is also worth seeing (Park Avenue between 111th and 116th Streets).

LOWER EAST SIDE. This district is not so easily defined, but generally speaking it borders the north side of 14th Street, the western side of Fifth Avenue and in the south the charming offices of the New York Justice Department on Centre Street. It was in this area that many newly-arrived immigrants first settled before moving on to establish today's distinctly ethnic quarters of New York. In the middle of the last century, the Lower East Side was the most densely populated

Above: View of south Manhattan from the Brooklyn Bridge. Below: The quay in Battery Park.

excellent bookshops providing an atmosphere like a small university town. **Montgomery Place** probably boasts the best surviving example of nineteenth century townhouse architecture from New York City.

ROCKEFELLER CENTER. This was New York's first highrise office building complex. Built in the 1930s, it stretches between Fifth and Sixth Avenues and between 50th and 53rd Streets and remains a favourite tourist attraction. The pedestrianised Rockefeller Plaza, with its fountains and greenery, provides a restful retreat from the bustle of nearby Fifth Avenue. A favourite meeting place is the golden Prometheus Statue, with its outdoor café in summer, plus boutiques and galleries.

Another attraction is the **"Big Apple" Multi-Media Show** on the ground floor of the McGraw Hill Building, where forty-five simultaneous colour projections will send your senses reeling. For a

Park Slope is a residential area favoured by intellectuals, young families and bohemians. Within the boundaries of Prospect Park West, Sixth and Flatbush Avenues and Garfield Place there are cafés, vegetarian restaurants, bars and

breathtaking view of New York, as well as a good meal, allow yourself to be catapulted by lift to the **Rainbow Room** at the top of the RCA Building (Radio Corporation of America). *29, 46*

STATEN ISLAND FERRY. This is one of the prettiest and cheapest tourist attractions of New York. The half-hour journey from the Staten Island Ferry Terminal, near Battery Park, to Staten Island costs the same as it has for decades – twenty-five cents. The free return trip provides a priceless view of Manhattan and Brooklyn. The ferry passes close to the Statue of Liberty.

STATUE OF LIBERTY. In good weather, the observation platform at the top of the most famous landmark in New York and the United States offers an excellent view of Manhattan and Brooklyn. The Statue of Liberty is reached via Battery Park at the south end of Manhattan.

TRIBECA. Short for Triangle Below Canal Street, several former warehouses provide a home today for a variety of unusual bars and clubs catering to the eccentric elements of the Downtown crowd. Tribeca is located in a triangular area bordered by Canal Street, Hudson Street and West Broadway near the Hudson River.

U. N. QUARTER. The impression from television pictures is simply of the buildings on the East River which accommodate the General Assembly of the United Nations. But there is much more: tours, exhibitions, souvenir shops and one of the most cultivated green spaces in New York, the **UN Park**. Noteworthy sights include the **Polish Consulate** built in the style of a miniature French château (37th Street, near Madison Avenue); the **Morgan Library** with its valuable handwritten manuscripts and books (36th Street/Madison Avenue); **Tudor City**, a tiny enclave built in the 1930s in the Tudor style (43rd Street); the view from the cable railway to **Roosevelt Island** (Second Avenue/59th Street) and the skyscrapers of midtown Manhattan; and the **Abigail Adam Smith Museum** with its collection of everyday possessions from the last century. The Smith Museum is inside an eighteenth century country house,

East 54th Street) long enough, you might catch of a glimpse of Gloria Vanderbilt, the Kissingers or Jackie Onassis. This is where the most expensive apartments are located.

But east of Third Avenue, the city's environment is not so elegant: this is where single people and professional working couples live. The bars and restaurants here cater to the younger, but no less joyful guests.

In Yorkville, on 86th Street, there is a mixture of Mexican, Japanese, Chinese, Thai and Afghan restaurants, as well as a few cafés and cake shops catering to the last survivors of the district's German community.

On **East 78th Street**, in the area of Third Avenue up to **Cherokee Place**, there is an example of successful town planning,

Above: Columbus and Columbus Circle. Below: George Washington overlooks Wall Street.

wedged between two garages (421 East 61st Street, near New York Avenue).

UPPER EAST SIDE. This is Manhattan's richest, "whitest" and safest district – the domain of the jet set, the preserve of the successful and the super-rich. A typical home (owned, not rented) has ten rooms, a canopied entrance and a uniformed doorman to whistle a taxi and take the dirty washing to the laundry. **Beekman Place** (49th to 51st Streets) and **Sutton Place** (53rd to 59th Streets) are oases of rural peace and quiet. If you stand outside **River House** (435 East 52nd Street) or **St. James Towers** (415

a harmonious union of home and work place.

UPPER WEST SIDE. A quick look at this popular area west of Central Park will tell you why it is known as "Yupper West Side". This is the location of the **Lincoln Center, Columbia University** and the legendary delicatessen **"Zabar's"** (2245 Broadway/80th Street).

Many large old houses crowd the area around Central Park West, among them the **Dakota Building** (East 72nd Street), where Roman Polanski's film "Rosemary's Baby" was produced and where John Lennon lived.

Columbia and Amsterdam Avenues are lined with cinemas, food, book and antique shops, street cafés and restaurants – another reason for this district's attractiveness.

Further interesting sights are **Grant's Tomb**, the controversial mausoleum of General Grant (Riverside Drive/122nd Street) and the American Province College campus of **Columbia University** on Morningside Heights (110th to 125th Street).

WALL STREET/FINANCIAL DISTRICT.

The first Dutch settlers on the southern tip of Manhattan built a protective stockade across the island against attacks from Indian natives. The line of this stockade is today's Wall Street, the heart of the American financial market. Apart from the **New York Stock Exchange** *(27)*, where regular tours take place and **Federal Hall** (today a museum), other attractions include: **South Street Seaport Museum** on the East River; the **Whitney Museum of American Art** (26 Wall Street, corner of Nassau Street); the historic **Trinity Church** built between 1839 and 1846 (Wall Street, corner with Broadway); and **St. Paul's Chapel**, Manhattan's oldest church, built between 1764 and 1766 (Broadway, near Fulton Street).

Enthusiasts of "high tech" architecture will be fascinated with the four towers of the **World Finance Center**, where stock and security bond dealers work around the clock. The pedestrian zone around **Nassau Street** is a shopping paradise.

Those who like heights can go to the 107th floor of the **World Trade Center** *(34/35)* – the world's second tallest building after Chicago's Sears Tower – and experience dinner 438 yards/400 metres) up in the **Windows on the World Restaurant**.

ZOOS.
New York has many zoos. The **Bronx Zoo** is one of the biggest in the world (reached by subway lines 2 or 5), and the **Botanic Garden** opposite is also worth a visit. **Central Park** has a small zoo with an enclosure where some animals can be stroked, and a section where polar bears can be observed under water. The **New York Aquarium**, near the Astroland Fun Park on Coney Island, has sharks, whales and a dolphin show. It is open from May to September.

The twin towers of the World Trade Center.

LIST OF SOURCES AND ILLUSTRATIONS

Djuna Barnes, *Greenwich Village as It Is.* New York: People's Magazine, (October) 1916.

Simone De Beauvoir, *America Day by Day.* Trans. Patrick Dudley. London: Gerald Duckworth & Company Ltd, 1952. (*L'Amerique au Jour le Jour.* Paris: Editions Paul Morihien, 1950).

Abraham Cahan, *The Rise of David Levinsky.* New York: Harper & Row, 1960.

Edward Corsi, "Arriving in America", in *In the Shadow of Liberty: The Chronicle of Ellis Island.* New York: The Macmillan Company, 1935.

Theodore Dreiser, *The Color of a Great City.* New York: Boni and Liveright Inc., 1923.

Rudolph Fisher, *The City of Refuge.* New York: Atlantic Monthly, 1925.

Zelda Fitzgerald, "A Millionaire's Girl", in *Bits of Paradise.* London: Penquin Group, 1973.

Marita Golden, *Migrations of the Heart.* New York: The Anchor Press, 1983.

Brander Matthews, *Vignettes of New York.* New York: Harper & Brothers, 1894.

Isaac Bashevis Singer, *Enemies: A Love Story.* London: Penguin Books, 1972.

Dan Wakefied, "A Trip to the Moon", in *Island in the City: The World of Spanish Harlem.* Boston: Houghton Mifflin Company, 1959.

We would like to thank all copyright holders and publishers for their kind permission to publish. Despite intensive efforts on our part, in a few cases we were not able to find out who the copyright holders are. Those to whom this applies are asked to contact us.

© Diercke Kartographie, Westermann Verlag, Braunschweig: map on page 48.
The district map in the right hand corner on pape 48 was drawn by Peter Schmid, Munich.

All other photographs: Detlef Ihlenfeldt, Bremen.

DESTINATION NEW YORK
WINDSOR BOOKS INTERNATIONAL, 1992

© 1989 Verlag C. J. Bucher GmbH,
Munich and Berlin
Translation: Graham Lees
Editor: Karen Lemiski
Anthology: Carmel Finnan, Karen Lemiski
All rights reserved
Printed and bound in Germany
ISBN 1 874111 04 9